Stunning Spreads

Stunning Spreads

Easy Entertaining with Cheese, Charcuterie, Fondue & Other Shared Fare

Chrissie Nelson Rotko

creator of OffTheEatenPathBlog.com

Skyhorse Publishing

Skyhorse Publishing books may be purchased in bulk at special discounts for sales promotion, corporate gifts, fund-raising, or educational purposes. Special editions can also be created to specifications. For details, contact the Special Sales Department, Skyhorse Publishing, 307 West 36th Street, 11th Floor, New York, NY 10018 or info@skyhorsepublishing.com.

Skyhorse® and Skyhorse Publishing® are registered trademarks of Skyhorse Publishing, Inc.®, a Delaware corporation.

Visit our website at www.skyhorsepublishing.com.

10 9 8 7 6

Library of Congress Cataloging-in-Publication Data is available on file.

Cover design by Daniel Brount
Cover photo by Chrissie Nelson Rotko

Print ISBN: 978-1-5107-5522-2
Ebook ISBN: 978-1-5107-5523-9

Printed in China

To Mom, Dad, and Katie: Thank you for always being my biggest supporters and cheerleaders. I'm so lucky to have you on my team. You've always believed in me and told me that if I worked hard, I could do anything. This book wouldn't have happened without your love and encouragement.

To AJ: You are the best hand model, taste tester, dishwasher, and partner I could have ever asked for. Thank you for all of the time, energy, and patience you've dedicated to this project and our family. And thank you for all of the joy, laughter, and love you've brought into my life.

These tiny paragraphs can't convey to my four favorite people how lucky I am to have all of you and how much I love you.

Table of Contents

Introduction

I love food.

I'm pretty sure you love food too, which is why you bought this book.

There's so much to love about good food—flavor, taste, fuel, and nourishment—that are important elements of our daily lives. But one of my favorite things is the social aspect surrounding it; sharing great meals with family and friends, and how even the simplest of meals can be about gathering and bringing people together.

It's the homemade lemon birthday cake my grandmother, Baba, would make for me every year to celebrate another milestone (sometimes, going to great lengths of traveling with her cake stand cradled in her lap on DC's Metro to make sure it was safely delivered to the suburbs). It's rolling out Grandma Vera's sugar cookies and pressing Norwegian sandbakkels into tins with my mom while Nat King Cole or Bing Crosby croons holiday favorites in the background. (We even packed our sandbakkel tins and rolling pin in our suitcases the year our family spent Christmas in Hawaii!) It's my sister, mom, aunt, and me churning out one hundred mini cherry and pecan pies three days before Katie's wedding, chatting and laughing around Mom's kitchen table while we mixed up pie filling and layered tiny lattice pie crusts. A lot of my favorite memories (I have some savory memories too, but all those that stick out in my mind are sweet) feature food, and my family and friends gathered around a table, talking, laughing, and eating.

My husband, AJ, and I are now creating memories around our own kitchen table. We love having our friends and family over for everything from the holidays (this will be our fourth year hosting our family for Thanksgiving) to something more low-key like game night or watching a football game on TV. But I hate all the hubbub that comes with hosting: the prep, the cleanup, and the fact that the host inevitably ends up stuck in the kitchen rather than having fun and spending time with their guests. So, when it comes to hosting, I like to make it as hassle-free as possible.

For a long time, I was intimidated and overwhelmed by in-home entertaining. When it came to feeding guests, it was hard for me to achieve a balance between frantically getting stuck and stressed in the kitchen and just mailing it in by opening a bag of chips, popping a jar of salsa, and calling it a day. It wasn't until I learned to balance what I could make from scratch, what I could rely on from the store, plus a healthy dose of timing and what I'm going to call "artful arranging" (making things look nice and delicious and appealing on a plate or platter) that I gained confidence when it came to entertaining.

So, what is that perfect balance? I like to call it "easy entertaining." Making delicious and beautiful spreads for your guests doesn't have to be daunting, difficult, or time-consuming. By making a few easy-to-follow, uncomplicated recipes ahead of time, and then mixing those things with a few high-quality, store-bought snacks and ingredients, you can create a stunning spread that both your guests, and you, can enjoy. Because after all, your guests are in your home to, guess what, spend time with you. The delicious food is an added bonus!

Stunning Spreads features seventy-five of my favorite recipes for easy entertaining. These approachable recipes covering everything from cheese and snack boards, to fondues, dips, snacks, appetizers, and cocktails are ones I make in my own kitchen all the time when we invite people over. All of these recipes can be easily prepped and cooked ahead of time, so when guests arrive, the focus can be on them instead of the food. And, most importantly, the host isn't chained to the kitchen.

What I really wanted to do with this book was to show you that entertaining doesn't have to be intimidating or overwhelming, and to give you the confidence to create delicious food for your family and friends. I want to help you create those same fond food memories with people gathered around your table talking, laughing, and eating food that you prepared and made for them with love.

Here's to new savory and sweet food memories for you and your loved ones,

Chrissie

Chapter 1

Cheese, Charcuterie & Snack Board Basics

Cheese, charcuterie, and snack boards are one of my favorite ways to feed and impress my guests. They are well-suited for basically any occasion from a quiet date night at home, book club or girls' night in, to a dinner party or big holiday bash because they are versatile, customizable, colorful, and can cater to a wide variety of people's tastes all on one plate. Plus, they are really easy and often quick to make. (We're talking putting it all together in less than twenty minutes easy.)

This chapter covers everything when it comes to composing a beautifully crafted and delicious cheese, charcuterie, or snack board: what type of boards and platters to use, what other serving ware or utensils you need, what kind of cheese and other foods to serve and how much you need, and how to put it all together to make it look beautiful and appetizing. Use these tips and tricks to help you make a well-rounded, stunning spread for your guests.

What kind of boards or surfaces should I use?

You know you need something to put your cheeses and other board components on . . . but you don't own a "cheese board." That's okay! You probably own something totally acceptable to build a platter or board on because any flat surface will do! Platters and boards come in a lot of different shapes, sizes, and materials. Any size, as large as a serving platter, or small as a dinner plate, is perfect to build a platter or board. Any shape, rectangular, square, round, oval, or more out of the box, like your favorite animal or home state, is perfect to build a platter or a board. Any material, wood, marble, slate, metal, glass, plastic, or ceramic is perfect to build a platter or board. This could be anything from a wooden or slate cheese board, to a marble platter, or even a baking sheet pan or muffin tin. That glass platter you were gifted for your wedding eight years ago that's buried in the back of a closet somewhere? Dig it out and build a board on it. Have a big countertop or tabletop? Lay down some butcher paper and build a board for a crowd . . . it will make for easy cleanup later!

What other serving ware or utensils do I need for easy entertaining and to make the boards and other recipes featured in this book?

When it comes to making cheese and snack boards, I always like to have a variety of different containers on hand, like small bowls, jars, dishes, and cups. Small containers are perfect for separating different components of a platter or board as well as holding the liquid ingredients of a board (like honey, preserves, sauces, dips, or olives) so they don't run all over the board and into the other ingredients.

While you could use regular knives or utensils, I recommend investing in a set of cheese knives. They are pretty affordable, usually have unique and pretty details that add to the look of a platter or board, and also give you a practical serving tool for each piece of cheese to prevent too much flavor mixing. You'll also want serving utensils like spoons and tongs for other board ingredients, as well as utensils that will help your guests eat, like forks, toothpicks, or skewers.

This book features both savory and sweet fondues (there's a whole fondue chapter on page 47), and that's because I think fondue can be a really fun way to serve a meal to any size group and can be either the central focus or a unique component of a platter or board. In order to keep fondue warm for your guests to enjoy over a few hours as they dip and chat, and then chat and dip some more, consider using a fondue pot with a candle or gas element or a small or medium sized slow cooker. Both are designed to give off gradual heat and keep cheese and chocolate fondue warm.

Speaking of fondue, the quickest and easiest way I've found to make fondue is on the stove in a double boiler and then transferring it to a fondue pot or slow cooker for serving. This prevents fondues and warm dips from breaking or separating. You can create a makeshift double boiler with a saucepan and a heatproof mixing bowl, or buy one at the store. Another tool I love for dips, sauces, and fondues is an immersion blender. This tool will save you time by blending your dips, sauces, and fondues right in the pot you cooked them in rather than having to transfer them back and forth to a blender or food processor.

Last, we always stock our home bar with a cocktail shaker and a cocktail muddler. Sure, a wooden spoon or spatula will get the job done when it comes to mixing fruit and other cocktail ingredients, but a muddler is inexpensive and specifically designed to muddle or mash fruits, herbs, and spices at the bottom of the glass to release their flavors.

What kind of cheese should I put on my cheese board?

For a cheese lover like me, narrowing down what kind of cheese to use is the hardest part of building a cheese board. My goal every time I build a cheese platter or board is to feature a variety. What kind of variety? Well, cheeses can widely vary when it comes to color, texture, flavor, aroma, taste, style, and even type of milk, so pick ones that embody different characteristics and stand out from the others on your board so you can give your guests plenty of different options.

Texture: soft, spreadable, semi-soft, soft ripened, drippy, hard, creamy, crumbly

Flavor: fresh, aged, blue, flavor added, milky, strong, goat, stinky, funky, salty, spicy, sweet, nutty, sharp, briny, buttery

Color: orange, white, blue, golden, cream, cloudy, yellow

Aroma: milky, mild, moldy, pungent, stinky, earthy, nutty, fruity

Type of milk: cow, sheep, goat, water buffalo

Some of my favorite cheeses to feature on a cheese board: goat cheese, chèvre, feta, ricotta, Stilton, Gorgonzola, Roquefort, Brie, Camembert, muenster, Gouda, cheddar, Monterey or pepper jack, Gruyère, burrata, mozzarella, and Manchego.

It's always good to include one or two more approachable cheeses on a cheese platter or board. Cheeses like cheddar, Swiss, Gouda, or even Brie are more well-known and can cater to the less adventurous eaters in your group. Just because they are more familiar or approachable doesn't mean they aren't delicious! And just because it's recommended that you serve a variety of cheeses, it doesn't mean that you have to! Try building a board surrounding one cheese type, like the Ultimate Cheddar Board (see recipe on page 14), or UnBrielievable Board (see recipe on page 17), one texture, or even one or a few colors, like the Red, White & Blue Board (see recipe on page 18).

How much cheese should I serve?

For an appetizer board, include about one to two ounces of cheese per person. For a more filling board or main course, feature about three to four ounces of cheese per person.

Include anywhere from three to five types on cheese on a board to give guests a wide variety of options and to showcase different textures, flavors, and colors. For a crowd, you could use up to seven different cheeses, but I find three to five to be the sweet spot.

Do I have to buy expensive cheese?

No! The key to a great cheese board is including a variety of tasty cheeses and ingredients. Delicious, quality cheese doesn't have to be expensive and there are a few ways you can make a cheese board more budget friendly: compare prices at a variety of grocery stores before purchasing; buy cheese or other ingredients that are on sale; or even consider making a less expansive platter or board with a lesser variety of ingredients like two kinds of cheeses, one kind of meat, one type of fruit, and one variety of nuts or crunch.

What else should be on a cheese board?

While cheese is the star of the show on a cheese board, you also need plenty of supporting actors or accompanying bites to round out your cheese board: like meats, fruits, vegetables, breads and crackers, nuts, and other condiments. Similar to choosing cheese, you want an assortment of cheese-pairing foods that showcase different textures (soft and crunchy), flavors (sweet and salty), and colors that both complement and contrast the cheeses you're serving.

Meat: The principles of choosing cheese are the same for meat; you want a variety of flavors, colors, and textures. Choose two to three different types of meat. Some of the varieties I like to include on cheese boards are: prosciutto, salami, peppered or herb-crusted salami, chorizo, ham, turkey, sausage, or bacon. If you're a vegetarian, don't fear! You don't need meat to make a good cheese board. There are a lot of yummy alternatives to meat that you can include like roasted chickpeas, caramelized onions, artichokes, hummus, or other dips.

Breads/crackers/carbs: Carbs in any form are perfect for smearing, dipping, and piling high with cheese, meat, honey, preserves, or other goodies you have on your cheese board. Serve breads, crackers, crisps, pretzels, crostini, or bread sticks that have a neutral flavor, so they don't overpower or compete with the flavor of the cheese or other condiments.

Fruits/vegetables: I always love to include what I call a fresh element on my cheese boards, which usually comes in the form of a fruit or vegetable (or both). Produce can round out your cheese board, so pick fruits and vegetables that are in season and pair and balance with the flavors of the cheese on your board.

Condiments/dips/spreads: Things like honey, jams, preserves, olives, mustards, hummus, tapenades, and salsas can really bring out the flavors of the cheeses and other ingredients on your board. There are several recipes for homemade dips, condiments, and spreads in this book including Fresh Basil Pesto (see recipe on page 92), Bourbon Apple Butter (see recipe page on page 103), Marinated Olives (see recipe on page 138), Whipped Ricotta (see recipe on page 100), and more. Pair the flavors of your featured cheeses and fruit and vegetable components with homemade condiments and spreads or your favorite store-bought ones.

Nuts: Nuts add a great texture and final touch to a board; I love using them not only to add some crunch but also to fill in blank or empty spaces around the platter or board. My favorite nuts to use include walnuts, pecans, almonds, marcona almonds, pistachios, cashews, hazelnuts, pumpkin seeds, or peanuts. You could even use white or dark chocolate for crunch and a little sweet component.

Garnish: Fresh herbs add a wonderful aroma and pop of color to any cheese, charcuterie, or snack board. Think about using herbs like rosemary, basil, thyme, sage, or dill, or even edible flowers, depending on the season.

How much of everything else should I serve?

For an appetizer board, include one to two ounces of meat, three to six pieces of fruits and vegetables, one to two condiments, and one to two tablespoons of nuts or crunch per person. For a more filling board or main course, include three to four ounces of meat, five to ten pieces of fruit or vegetables, and three to four tablespoons of nuts or crunch per person.

Does a platter or board have to focus on cheese?

No! In fact, not every platter or board you make needs to include cheese. Plenty of boards in this book focus on or showcase ingredients other than cheese like the Summer Grilled Fruit & Veggie Board (see recipe on page 21), Elevate your Tailgate Board (see recipe on page 26), Colorful Crudités Platter (see recipe on page 30), Brunch Board (see recipe on page 38), Fruit Platter (see recipe on page 33), and Build-Your-Own Bloody Mary Board (see recipe on page 41). When conceptualizing and creating a board, think about the focus of your board, whether it be on a theme or one or two essential items. Then, build your board in order to showcase those items or that theme.

How do I arrange a platter or board to make it look nice?

Let's compose a board step-by-step so you can see how I build and arrange a cheese or snack board. These step-by-step photos feature the Flavors of Fall Board (see recipe page on page 25).

I start arranging my board with the items that take up the most room, which is most often small bowls or dishes that hold snacks, jams, and jellies.

Then, I place the cheese, spreading it out into different areas of the board so the flavors don't mix and there is space to put other elements near each piece of cheese.

Next I move on to the meat, fanning and grouping it in different places across the board.

I then add any fruits, vegetables, or other snacks I'm going to feature. I finish up a board by filling in any blank spots with nuts and garnish.

As I'm building my board, I make sure to place complementary flavors near each other.

Other serving suggestions

- Serve cheese at room temperature. Take cheese out of the fridge thirty minutes to one hour before serving and allow them to come to room temperature. (I love to build a cheese board and put on the final touches about an hour before my guests arrive and then just leave them out for serving.) Serving cheese at room temperature showcases cheese's best flavors, textures, and aromas, and the cheese will taste more complex, nuanced, and delicious.

- Tell guests to sample the cheese from mild to strongest or most pungent.

- Encourage guests to create the perfect bite by combining different elements of the board.

- Use a separate cheese knife for each cheese so the flavors are kept distinct and aren't mingling.

- People like to know what they will be tasting before taking a bite, so label each cheese to let your guests know about their different choices.

- Cut some of the cheese in advance and then arrange it on your board. Pre-cutting or slicing some of the cheese will keep your board or platter tidier by making it easier for your guests to dig right in and enjoy the board without having to cut anything, and giving them an example of how each type of cheese should be sliced. Pre-cut each type or variety of cheese in a different way on the board whether in wedges, slices, strips, cubes, chunks, or crumbles.

- If you are including a certain ingredient (like a vegetable, fruit, jam, or other spread) because it pairs well with a specific cheese, place the two items next to each other to visually show people they are meant to be eaten together.

- Offer a variety of savory and sweet ingredients on a board; both will bring out the flavor of the cheese in different ways.

Chapter 2

Boards & Platters

Cheese, charcuterie, and snack boards are the epitome of easy entertaining. By doing some prep work up front, you can have a gorgeous, colorful, and delicious display of different flavors and ingredients for your guests. Beyond boards and platters being total tablescape showstoppers, what I love about them is they take serving at a party or gathering out of the equation because guests can just help themselves.

A board or platter is perfect for any season, like the Summer Grilled Fruit & Veggie Board (see recipe on page 21) and the Winter Cheese Board (see recipe on page 29), or any occasion, like the Brunch Board (see recipe page on page 38) or Elevate Your Tailgate Board (see recipe on page 26). Some don't even need a special reason or season to be made. We love snacking on the UnBrielievable Board (see recipe on page 17) for an easy dinner at home, making a Dessert Board (see recipe on page 42) when we have a sweet tooth craving, or putting out a Sweet & Salty Snack Board (see recipe on page 34) when we host a few friends for game night or book club or to just come over and hang out.

I've been making cheese and snack boards for a few years now and often turn to them as the main menu item for anything I'm planning, from a date night at home with just the two of us, to a light lunch on Thanksgiving to give our families something to munch on. I wanted to feature board recipes in this book that would become staples in your house year after year and event after event (of course, I always encourage you to include your own unique spins and twists to these recipes to really make them yours).

In creating each of the boards and platters in this book, I thought about a few things:

- **Accessibility of ingredients.** How easy it would be for you to go to your local grocery store and find and buy the board or platter ingredients.

- **Seasonality of ingredients.** It makes sense for tomatoes, berries, and fresh watermelon to be the stars of summer themed boards when they are in season, and fall and winter fruit and vegetables like squash, apples, and pomegranates to be featured on, you guessed it, fall and winter boards. Not that you can't put a tomato or watermelon on a winter board, but fresh, good tasting watermelon is a lot easier to find at my local store in July than it is in January.

- **Amount of work involved.** In trying to stay true to my philosophy of easy entertaining, most of these boards can be composed in less than thirty minutes, including the prep and cook time for any fruits, veggies, condiments, or other components that need to be chopped, sliced, diced, or cooked. But as always, there's an exception to the rule, so some boards may take a little bit longer to put together, but I promise you they're worth it. If there's a recipe that requires you to cook several different components (like the Elevate Your Tailgate Board on page 26) I suggest making everything a day ahead of time and then storing in the fridge and reheating (if needed) as you put your board together. That way you can break your prep work up, and the board will still come together easily in less than half an hour.

- **Design of the board.** Not only are all of the boards and platters pretty and visually attractive, but ingredients are placed where they are to create color and texture contrast and harmony, as well as to pair flavors (more on flavors below).

- **Flavors of the board.** I did a *lot* of research (if you added up my research hours it would probably turn into days and I am not being hyperbolic) before composing the boards regarding different flavor profiles and flavor pairings of the different board components (cheeses, meats, fruits, vegetables, nuts, condiments, and anything else).

For each board in this chapter, I would get an idea and research potential ingredients based on the board's theme (whether they need to be seasonal or color coordinated or in one food group), and the complementary and contrasting ingredients and flavor profiles. The goal with my research was to create boards that could be easily replicated at home with ingredients that tasted good together. Every single element on all of the boards and platters in this book are there for a reason, because it is not only delicious on its own, but complements the entire board and adds something to elevate the board both in flavor and appearance.

Even with all the talk about days of research, flavor profiles, pairings, and intentional ingredients, it is okay for you to make small substitutions on these boards. In fact, I encourage it! There are no hard and fast rules when it comes to creating boards and platters, so if you simply don't like an ingredient, or forgot to pick it up from the store, or you're just trying to create a platter or board with things you already have in your fridge and pantry, then feel free to make any creative substitutions you want or see necessary. If absolutely no one at your party is going to eat blue cheese, then don't put blue cheese on the board! Or better yet, follow my board basics guide in Chapter 1 and create a board that's all your own!

Recipe List

Easy Cheese & Charcuterie Board

SERVES: 6–8 as an appetizer

Prep time: 5 minutes | Active time: 10–15 minutes | Total time: 20 minutes

This recipe should be used as a guide to help you compose and put together an easy and elegant cheese and charcuterie board. Always remember that the options are endless when it comes to flavor and color combinations of cheese and charcuterie, so feel free to substitute or customize your own board depending on your preferences, what is available at your local store, or what you have in your refrigerator and pantry. Don't like goat cheese? That's okay! No apricots available? No problem! Cater to you and your guests' own tastes and preferences to create a totally custom appetizer that is all your own.

INGREDIENTS

4 ounces cheddar cheese, sliced

4 ounces Manchego cheese, sliced

3 ounces goat cheese, sliced

3 ounces Brie, sliced

1 green apple, sliced

2–4 apricots, halved

4 ounces (about 16–20) cherries

3 small bunches grapes

8–10 mini bell peppers, sliced

½ cup Marinated Olives (see recipe on page 138)

3 ounces prosciutto, sliced

3 ounces salami, sliced

crackers

¼ cup walnuts

¼ cup pecans

INSTRUCTIONS

1. About an hour before your guests arrive, remove cheese from refrigerator and unwrap so it can come to room temperature.

2. Prepare your cheese, fruit, and vegetables.

3. Place olives in a bowl and onto your board.

4. Arrange your cheeses. Place cheeses on your board or serving platter. Spread cheeses out to different areas or corners of the platter to create a more visually pleasing board and so their flavors don't mix.

5. Arrange your meats. Fan out slices of prosciutto and salami and place in different areas of your platter or board.

6. Place crackers in different areas of the board near each cheese. You can also serve crackers on a separate plate, bowl, or board on the side.

7. Place fruits, veggies, and other snacks in various places throughout the board, filling visible space on the board as you go.

8. Fill in remaining gaps of your board with walnuts and pecans.

9. Serve and enjoy! As cheese and other elements get low, replenish with extras that you are storing in the fridge.

Ultimate Cheddar Snack Board

SERVES: 4–6

Prep time: 10 minutes | Active time: 10 minutes | Total time: 20 minutes

Cheddar is a well-loved hard cheese that can range in color, flavor, and texture (depending how you use it), so why not create a board showcasing cheddar in a few different ways? The Ultimate Cheddar Snack Board stars four different types of cheddar: medium, sharp, extra sharp, and shredded. This board is perfect for the cheddar lovers in your life or as a great introductory, approachable cheese board for guests who may not be that familiar with or prefer the strong and distinct flavors of more unique cheeses.

INGREDIENTS

4 ounces medium cheddar cheese

4 ounces sharp cheddar cheese

4 ounces extra sharp cheddar cheese

4 ounces Pimento Cheese (see recipe on page 75)

½–1 cup Marinated Olives (see recipe on page 138)

10 ounces salami

1 green apple, sliced

2 bunches green grapes

handful of dried or fresh figs

½ cup roasted red peppers

½ cup dried cranberries

½ cup marcona almonds

½ cup Cinnamon Sugar Walnuts (see recipe on page 145)

½ cup dark chocolate

assortment of pretzels and crackers

INSTRUCTIONS

1. Slice cheeses into easy to grab and serve slices or wedges.

2. Make pimento cheese according to recipe instructions and place in a small dish.

3. Make marinated olives according to recipe instructions and place in a small dish.

4. Arrange your board. Start with placing a bowl of olives on the board.

5. Spread out the cheeses into four different locations around the board.

6. Place your salami and flower or fan it out in two different places on your board.

7. Add your fruits, fanning out apples and placing bunches of grapes and figs on your board.

8. Add roasted red peppers.

9. Finish with dried cranberries, almonds, cinnamon sugar walnuts (make according to recipe instructions), and dark chocolate and serve with pretzels and crackers.

UnBrielievable Board

SERVES: 4–6 as an appetizer

Prep time: 20 minutes | Active time: 20 minutes | Total time: 40 minutes

This UnBrielievable Board features ingredients that complement Brie's luscious, delicate flavor and velvety texture, plus plenty of French bread just begging for a smooth smear of soft, creamy Brie. On a board like this dedicated to just one type of cheese, you want to complete the spread with fruits, vegetables, snacks, and condiments (accoutrements, if you will, since Brie is a French cheese after all) that enhance but don't overwhelm the flavor of Brie, because the accompaniments shouldn't compete with the cheese!

INGREDIENTS

8 ounces Baked Brie (see Cranberry-Walnut Baked Brie recipe on page 87) or Grilled Brie (see recipe on page 84)

½ cup Honey-Roasted Almonds (see recipe on page 146)

¼ –½ cup caramelized (1 whole) red or white onion

4-ounce wedge/small wheel plain Brie

10 slices baguette or French bread (more for serving)

5 figs, halved

1 apple, sliced

½–1 cup blueberries

2 ounces sun-dried tomatoes

½ cup pistachios

rosemary, for garnish

crackers (optional)

INSTRUCTIONS

1. Make baked or grilled Brie according to recipe instructions.

2. Make honey-roasted almonds according to recipe instructions.

3. Caramelize the onion. Thinly slice one whole red or white onion lengthwise. Heat two tablespoons butter in a large pan or skillet over medium heat until melted and bubbling. Gradually add onions and cook, stirring occasionally, until onions are soft. Repeat until all onion slices have been added. Reduce heat to medium low or low and cook, stirring occasionally, for about 15 to 20 minutes until onions are super soft and caramelized. They should turn a light to medium brown color.

4. Place baked or grilled Brie on a small plate or piece of parchment paper (to prevent it from running all over your board and mixing flavors with other ingredients) and place on board.

5. Place wedge or small wheel of Brie on board.

6. Spoon onions into a small dish and place on board.

7. Add bread, fruit, tomatoes, and nuts to board where there is open space.

8. Add rosemary for garnish and serve with extra baguette, French bread, or your favorite crackers.

Red, White & Blue Board

SERVES: 8–10

Prep time: 10 minutes | Active time: 20 minutes | Total time: 30 minutes

This fresh and festive board features watermelon and a whole host of berries, each with a complementary cheese pairing, adding a patriotic pop to your summertime celebrations. Embrace the American flag color palette and serve this easy to prep showstopper as an appetizer at your Memorial Day, Fourth of July, or Labor Day cookouts, picnics, and pool parties.

INGREDIENTS

6 ounces Whipped Ricotta (see recipe on page 100)

6 slices watermelon

4 ounces Gorgonzola or other blue cheese

4 ounces blueberry-flavored chèvre or goat cheese (Note: you can substitute regular chèvre or goat cheese for the blueberry-flavored chèvre)

3 ounces Gouda cheese

2 ounces feta cheese

2 ounces (about 6 slices) salami

2 ounces (about 6 slices) capicola

8–10 strawberries

½ cup raspberries

½ cup blackberries

½ cup blueberries

water crackers

beet crackers

¼ cup sliced almonds

INSTRUCTIONS

1. Make whipped ricotta according to recipe instructions.

2. Place larger items like the bowl of whipped ricotta and watermelon slices on board.

3. Arrange the four cheeses on board, spreading them out on different areas so the flavors of each cheese are separated and don't mix.

4. Fan out salami and capicola and place in an empty space on board.

5. Arrange remaining fruit and crackers on the board.

6. Fill in the empty gaps on the board with sliced almonds.

Summer Grilled Fruit & Veggie Board

SERVES: 8–10 as an appetizer

Prep time: 15 minutes | Cook time: 20 minutes | Active time: 15 minutes | Total time: 50 minutes

This board is an ode to summer on a plate; packed with colorful and flavorful summer produce branded with marks from the kiss of a hot grill. No need to stick to these ingredients to a T; swap out whatever fruits and veggies are in season and available—different varieties of squash and peppers will taste great dipped in Roasted Garlic Dip (page 76) and if you've never grilled fruit . . . you have to try it! Grilling fruit caramelizes its natural sugars, adding a deliciously sweet and complex flavor.

INGREDIENTS FOR THE BOARD

2 peaches, halved, pitted

4–6 slices cantaloupe

10+ slices baguette

2 zucchinis, sliced into ¼-inch sticks

1 bunch asparagus, ends removed

1–2 summer squash, sliced into 1-inch round slices

12 shitake mushrooms, cleaned and stems removed

6–8 ounces Roasted Garlic Dip (see recipe on page 76)

4 ounces Bee Sting Chèvre Spread (see recipe on page 83)

2 tablespoons honey

INGREDIENTS FOR THE VEGETABLE MARINADE

½ cup olive oil

3–4 cloves garlic, minced

2 tablespoons lemon juice

½ teaspoon dried oregano

½ teaspoon dried basil

salt and pepper, to taste

INSTRUCTIONS

1. Light your grill and preheat to medium high heat.

2. Prepare your veggies.

3. Marinate your veggies. In a small bowl, whisk together the vegetable marinade ingredients. Place all veggies in a large bowl, baking dish, or plastic resealable bag and pour marinade over veggies. Let veggies marinate for at least 15 minutes in the refrigerator and up to 2 to 3 hours.

4. Prepare your fruit and bread. Brush sliced side of peaches and cantaloupe with olive oil. Brush both sides of bread with olive oil.

5. Grill the fruit and bread. Place peaches (olive oil side down), cantaloupe, and bread on the grill over medium high heat. Grill peaches for about 3 minutes until soft and grill marks appear, and remove. Grill cantaloupe for about 5 to 6 minutes (3 minutes per side) until grill marks appear, and remove. Grill bread about 1 minute per side until crispy.

6. Reduce grill heat to and grill your veggies. Grill zucchini for about 6 to 8 minutes until charred. Grill asparagus about 4 to 5 minutes until charred. Grill summer squash about 3 to 4 minutes per side until grill marks appear. Grill mushrooms about 2 minutes per side until softened.

7. Serve. Place bowl of roasted garlic dip, bowl of bee sting chèvre spread (make according to recipe instructions), and vessel of honey on serving platter or board. Arrange grilled fruit, veggies, and bread around the platter.

You can serve this grilled board warm or cold.

Caprese Salad Platter

SERVES: 8–10 as an appetizer, 4 as a main course

Prep time: 5 minutes | Cook time: 15 minutes | Total time: 20 minutes

This recipe is the perfect way to feature the tomatoes from your garden or farmers' market haul at summertime gatherings or soirées, but can also be enjoyed in the winter months (the colors of this platter are very holiday season appropriate). No matter the time of year you make this platter, make sure you are using high quality ingredients to showcase the simple flavors of the dish.

INGREDIENTS

4–8 ounces Heirloom Tomato Confit (see recipe on page 126)

3 tablespoons Fresh Basil Pesto (see recipe on page 92)

8 ounces burrata cheese

8 ounces mozzarella cheese (whole, slices, or small pearls)

5 medium to large heirloom tomatoes, sliced

1 pint cherry tomatoes

1–2 bunches basil

olive oil, balsamic vinegar, and crusty bread or crackers, for serving

INSTRUCTIONS

1. Make heirloom tomato confit and basil pesto according to recipe instructions.

2. Put heirloom tomato confit and basil pesto in two small bowls and place on serving platter or board.

3. Place burrata and mozzarella on a serving platter or board.

4. Arrange sliced tomatoes, cherry tomatoes, and basil around platter.

5. Serve with olive oil, balsamic vinegar, crusty bread or crackers, and extra basil if desired so guests can create their own perfect caprese bite.

Flavors of Fall Board

SERVES: 6–8 as an appetizer

Prep time: 5 minutes | Cook time: 30 minutes | Active time: 30 minutes |
Total time: 1 hour, 5 minutes

This cheese and charcuterie board perfectly complements the cooler temperatures and changing, colorful leaves that come as the seasons shift from summer into fall. The essence of fall is captured on this board not only through the reds, oranges, and yellows in its color palette, but also in its seasonal ingredients and flavors like apples, squash, carrots, pumpkins, and warming spices.

INGREDIENTS

½ cup Bourbon Apple Butter
(see recipe on page 103)

4 slices Candied Bacon (see
recipe on page 137), halved

1 medium delicata squash

2 small decorative pumpkins

5 ounces cheddar cheese

5 ounces Gruyère cheese

5 ounces herbed goat cheese

5 ounces herbed salami

1 apple, sliced

5–10 rainbow carrots

½–1 cup beet crackers or
crackers of your choice

½ cup hazelnuts

½ cup pumpkin seeds

¼ cup white chocolate chips

fresh sage leaves, for garnish

INSTRUCTIONS

1. Make the bourbon apple butter and candied bacon according to recipe instructions.

2. Roast the squash. Preheat the oven to 425°F. Scrub the outside of the squash with a brush under warm water. Cut off edges of squash and then cut in half lengthwise. Scoop out squash seeds. Cut squash into ½-inch slices (they will look like small half moons). Toss squash half moons in olive oil and season with salt and pepper. Spread out squash slices on a parchment paper–lined baking sheet in one even layer. Bake squash for 15 minutes, remove pan from oven, and flip each slice over. Bake for 15 more minutes until crispy and golden brown. Set squash aside to cool.

3. Assemble the board. On a rectangular wooden cutting board, marble board, or other platter, arrange larger items like decorative pumpkins and small jar of bourbon apple butter.

4. Slice cheddar and fan around one of the decorative pumpkins, and place Gruyère and herbed goat cheese on board.

5. Arrange candied bacon in the upper and lower corners of the board, and place salami around the other decorative pumpkin.

6. Place apple slices, carrots, squash, and crackers in different areas on the board.

7. Fill in the empty spaces on the board with hazelnuts, pumpkin seeds, and white chocolate chips.

8. Garnish with fresh sage leaves.

Elevate Your Tailgate Board

SERVES: 8–10 as an appetizer

Prep time: 10 minutes | Cook time: 10 minutes | Active time: 10 minutes | Total time: 30 minutes

This board is composed of my favorite game day snacks and will, as its name says, elevate your tailgate whether you're firing up the grill and tossing around a football in a parking lot at 9:00 a.m. or settling in to scream for four quarters from the comfort of your couch. This board features my tried and true easy appetizer recipes, like Roasted Jalapeño Poppers (see recipe on page 109), Slow-Cooker Party Meatballs (see recipe on page 113), Slow-Cooker Buffalo Turkey Meatballs (see recipe on page 114), Pepperoni Pinwheels (see recipe on page 117), Chile con Queso (see recipe on page 60), and Pimento Cheese (see recipe on page 75).

INGREDIENTS

8–10 Roasted Jalapeño Poppers (see recipe on page 109)

8–10 Slow-Cooker Party Meatballs (see recipe on page 113)

8–10 Slow-Cooker Buffalo Turkey Meatballs (see recipe on page 114)

8–10 Pepperoni Pinwheels (see recipe on page 117)

½ cup Chile con Queso (see recipe on page 60)

½ cup Pimento Cheese (see recipe on page 75)

2 bratwurst sausages, boiled, then grilled and sliced

1 bottle light beer (for the bratwurst)

½ white onion, sliced (for the bratwurst)

8 ounces cheddar cheese, cubed

8 ounces pepper jack cheese, cubed

carrot sticks

celery sticks

tortilla chips

2–3 tablespoons ranch dressing

INSTRUCTIONS

1. Make the roasted jalapeño poppers, party meatballs, buffalo turkey meatballs, pepperoni pinwheels, queso, and pimento cheese according to respective recipe instructions. These recipes can be made a day in advance and then reheated before putting together this board.

2. Make the bratwurst. Place brats in a deep pot. Pour beer over brats and add sliced onion. Bring brats to a boil. Once boiling, reduce heat to medium low and simmer until brats are cooked, about 10 minutes (they will turn an opaque gray color). Finish cooking the brats on the grill over medium or medium high heat, grilling them for a couple minutes on each side until brown. Slice brats.

3. Assemble the tailgate board. Using a twelve-well muffin pan, arrange poppers, meatballs, pinwheels, queso, cheese, bratwurst, veggies, and chips in each separate muffin well.

4. Serve board with a side of ranch.

5. Refill muffin wells as ingredients get low, or serve additional board components alongside the composed board.

Substitute your favorite game day snacks, dips, or appetizers for those used in this recipe to create a personalized spread to cheer on your favorite team!

Winter Cheese Board

SERVES: 8–10 as an appetizer

Active time: 30–40 minutes | Total time: 30–40 minutes

When creating seasonal cheese boards, using produce that is in season is a great way to celebrate the different types of fruits and vegetables that are available throughout the different months of the year. Creating a cheese board to reflect winter's produce and flavors is a little more difficult, because there are fewer fresh fruits and vegetables that grow and are harvested during the colder months. One of the brightest spots of winter produce is citrus fruit, which tend to ripen to their juiciest during winter. This board features a few unexpected but pleasant pairings to showcase winter's in-season produce.

INGREDIENTS

1 pomegranate

2 persimmons

½ cup honey

4 ounces White Stilton cheese

4 ounces aged Gouda cheese

4 ounces Gruyère cheese

4–8 ounces cranberry-flavored goat cheese (Note: you can substitute regular chèvre or goat cheese for the cranberry-flavored chèvre)

2 clementines, peeled and separated

1 pear, sliced

½ cup crackers (more for serving)

½ cup fresh cranberries, for garnish

½ cup hazelnuts

fresh rosemary, for garnish

INSTRUCTIONS

1. Cut open the pomegranate. Using a paring knife, remove the top (or flower) of the pomegranate by cutting around it at an angle. You want to cut into the pith, but not into the seeds. Next, score the sides of the fruit with your knife, cutting through the red rind and pith but not cutting into the seeds. Crack open the pomegranate using your thumbs and pulling the fruit apart gently. It will crack open along the lines you've scored in the skin.

2. Place the pomegranate, persimmons, and vessel of honey on the board or platter.

3. Arrange the four cheeses, spreading them out on different areas of the board so the flavors of each cheese are separated and don't intermingle or mix.

4. Arrange remaining fruit and crackers on the board.

5. Fill in the empty gaps on the board with cranberries and hazelnuts.

6. Garnish with rosemary.

Colorful Crudités Platter

SERVES: 6–8

Active time: 30 minutes

Vegetables just sound fancier when you call them crudités, right? Crudités, a French word meaning "raw things," are a traditional French appetizer featuring raw vegetables that are thinly sliced or cut into sticks and then served on a platter with a vinaigrette or dipping sauce. This board showcases crudités creativity in a few different ways with tons of color, a variety of veggies, and two unique dairy-free and vegan vegetable dips: Roasted Beet Dip (see recipe on page 95) and Curried White Bean Dip (see recipe on page 96).

INGREDIENTS

7 mini bell peppers or 1–2 bell peppers, sliced

9 small to medium carrots, peeled and sliced

1 cup broccoli florets

1 cup purple cauliflower florets

½–1 cup cherry heirloom tomatoes

1 cup snap peas

3 radishes, sliced

1 handful green beans

1 cucumber, sliced

8 ounces Roasted Beet Dip (see recipe on page 95)

8 ounces Curried White Bean Dip (see recipe on page 96)

INSTRUCTIONS

1. Pour roasted beet dip and curried white bean dip (make according to recipe instructions) into separate, small bowls. Place bowls apart on a serving platter or board.

2. Arrange vegetables on serving platter or board around the bowls of dip.

I prefer to use rainbow carrots, purple cauliflower, and heirloom tomatoes to add color to the platter, but orange carrots, white cauliflower, and tomatoes will do just fine.

Fruit Platter

SERVES: 8–10

Prep time: 20–25 minutes | Active time: 15–20 minutes | Total time: 35–45 minutes

Sliced fruit may seem simple but I really believe it can make a statement at any gathering. Pick fruits with a variety of different textures, flavors, and colors and then cut them in different ways to create an eye-catching, colorful, and delicious platter that can be served at everything from holidays to bridal and baby showers, or even as a snack or sweet treat for your kids.

INGREDIENTS

3 kiwis, divided

1 mango

8–12 ounces Piña Colada Fruit Dip (see recipe on page 99)

6 wedges watermelon

12 wedges pineapple

16 ounces strawberries

6 ounces raspberries

6 ounces blackberries

2 cups (15–20 pieces) cantaloupe, balled or cubed

INSTRUCTIONS

1. Lay two of the kiwis flat on the cutting board. Cut both ends off of each kiwi. With the kiwi still lying flat, insert your knife diagonally into the center of the kiwi, making a small, 45-degree angle slice. Then, insert the knife again beside the first cut, in the opposite diagonal direction, making a "v" shape. Continue cutting along the midline of the kiwi, creating a zigzag shape. Make sure the cuts are reaching the center of the fruit. Pull kiwi apart to separate. Lay the third kiwi flat on the cutting board and slice it thinly.

2. Place the mango vertically on the cutting board with the stem pointing up (it should look tall). Slice as close as you can to the pit, removing two halves or cheeks of the mango. Score each mango cheek into squares or cubes by cutting equally spaced vertical and horizontal lines, while making sure not to cut all the way through to the skin. Hold the scored mango cheek with two hands, and using your fingers, push the mango skin to invert the fruit so that the cubes pop out (making the mango cubes stick out like the quills of a hedgehog).

3. Arrange the fruit platter. Pour piña colada fruit dip (make according to recipe instructions) into a separate, small bowl and place in the upper part of the serving platter. Place the two mango cheeks on an angle at the center of the platter. Place a half a kiwi on each side of the mango. Fan the watermelon slices in the upper and lower corners of the platter. Line up about half of the pineapple slices just above and next to the mango. Fan the remaining pineapple slices around the bowl of piña colada fruit dip.

4. Start to fill in the remaining open spaces on the serving platter with the strawberries, raspberries, blackberries, cantaloupe, and remaining kiwi slices.

Sweet & Salty Snack Board

SERVES: 4–6

Active time: 10 minutes

I wanted to create a versatile snack board that would be perfect for any occasion: movie night, game night, book club, afternoon snacks, or even just when you need to get some food on the table in a pinch! The ingredients and flavors featured in this snack platter were picked for their complementary flavors (do not knock how a good aged Gouda tastes before or after some caramel until you try it!) but feel free to use this recipe as a template and create your own flavor combinations featuring your favorite snacks.

INGREDIENTS

1 cup Puppy Chow Popcorn (see recipe page on page 133)

1 cup Rosemary Garlic Popcorn (see recipe on page 130)

1 cup Bacon Fat Party Mix (see recipe on page 134)

4 ounces Pimento Cheese (see recipe on page 75)

½ cup Marinated Olives (see recipe on page 138)

1 cucumber, sliced

1 banana, sliced

½ cup raspberries

8 ounces aged Gouda cheese

1–2 bunches grapes

½ cup caramels, unwrapped

½ cup sweet and sour candy

crackers, for serving

INSTRUCTIONS

1. Make the puppy chow popcorn, rosemary garlic popcorn, party mix, pimento cheese, and marinated olives. All can be made and stored ahead of assembling this board.

2. Assemble the board. Using a twelve-well muffin pan, arrange all of the elements in individual wells. Refill muffin wells as ingredients get low, or serve additional board components alongside the composed board.

This board is a great way to empty what you have in your pantry!

Bagel Board

SERVES: 6–8

Prep time: 10 minutes | Active time: 20 minutes | Total time: 30 minutes

Saturday morning bagels were a ritual in our house growing up. My go-to order for ages was just a plain bagel with plain cream cheese (I know, so boring), but as I got older and I became a more adventurous eater, my bagel order also got more adventurous, branching into territories like sesame seeds, pumpernickel, everything bagels, scallion cream cheese, and eventually lox. Start your weekend off right gathered with loved ones and friends around this bagel board. It features all the makings of a delicious bagel with lox, including sliced tomatoes, red onion, capers, and (of course!) smoked salmon, plus three varieties of cream cheese.

INGREDIENTS

8 ounces Smoked Salmon Spread (see recipe on page 88)

4 ounces Herb Cream Cheese (see recipe on page 91)

¼ cup capers

4 ounces plain whipped cream cheese

2 Roma tomatoes, sliced

1 cucumber, sliced

½ red onion, sliced

8–10 ounces sliced smoked salmon

fresh dill, for garnish

6 bagels, sliced (or more, depending on your crowd)

INSTRUCTIONS

1. Make the smoked salmon spread and herb cream cheese (you can do this up to two days ahead of time).

2. Place capers, smoked salmon spread, herb cream cheese, and plain cream cheese in individual bowls. Arrange bowls on a serving platter or board.

3. Fan sliced tomatoes, cucumber, and onion around the board.

4. Fill in blank spaces on the board with smoked salmon.

5. Garnish with dill.

6. Serve with bagels (place bagels on the board if there is room)!

Brunch Board

Prep time: 10 minutes | Active time: 15–20 minutes | Total time: 25–30 minutes

My love of brunch blossomed in my early twenties, when I could use the meal as an excuse to get together with girlfriends, stuff my face full of the best of both breakfast and lunch, drink cocktails in the morning, and then after a sufficient amount of bottomless beverages, take a post-brunch nap on my living room couch. The hardest decision, for me at least, when it comes to brunch, is deciding between a sweet or savory meal. There are so many brunch foods I love to eat: French toast, pancakes, waffles, eggs Benedict, hash, sandwiches, avocado toast, I could go on and on and on, and I always have a hard time not ordering the entire menu . . . which is why I love this brunch board. If you can combine the best of both worlds when it comes to breakfast and lunch, why can't you combine the best sweet and savory elements too?

INGREDIENTS

8 pieces of Candied Bacon (see recipe on page 137) or cooked bacon, sliced in half

6 Egg Muffins (see recipe on page 129)

12 Cantaloupe & Prosciutto Skewers (see recipe on page 123)

2 avocados

6 waffles, homemade or store-bought

toast or sliced baguette (optional)

½ cup honey

½ cup maple syrup

12 ounces vanilla Greek yogurt

4 ounces strawberries

4 ounces raspberries

4 ounces blackberries

INSTRUCTIONS

1. Cook candied bacon according to recipe instructions. If not using candied bacon, fry bacon in a pan on the stovetop over medium heat until fully cooked (about 8 to 10 minutes).

2. Make egg muffins according to recipe instructions.

3. Make cantaloupe and prosciutto skewers according to recipe instructions.

4. Halve avocados and remove skin. Slice thinly but be careful not to mash or separate slices in order to serve avocado halves together on the board.

5. Lightly toast waffles and bread/toast, if using.

6. Pour honey and syrup into two separate vessels. Pour yogurt into a small bowl.

7. Arrange the brunch board. Fan waffles along the bottom half of the serving board or platter in an arch. Place vessel of syrup under the waffles, and vessel of honey just above the waffles. Place bowl with yogurt centered in the upper half of the serving board or platter. Arrange egg muffins in the top-left corner of the board or platter and the lower-left side just above the waffles. Arrange avocado halves and bacon near and around the egg muffins. Place cantaloupe and prosciutto skewers on the right side of the board around the honey vessel. Fill in blank spaces on the board with strawberries, blackberries, and raspberries.

8. Serve. Guests can put syrup, honey, yogurt, or fruit on top of their waffles, and can also build their own yogurt parfaits and avocado toast using the board ingredients.

Build-Your-Own Bloody Mary Board

SERVES: 6

Active time: 30 minutes | Total time: 30 minutes

The inspiration for this board came from my time in Wisconsin, where a build-your-own Bloody Mary bar was a regular Sunday morning activity (I think a Bloody Mary is the unofficial cocktail of the Badger State). Perfect to prep ahead of time for brunch or game day, this board features a wide variety of Bloody Mary garnishes and toppings (also known in Wisconsin as "the salad"). Go beyond basic celery and olives; we're talking everything from pickled veggies to shrimp, bacon, cheese cubes, and beef jerky, which allows your guests to mix and match their favorites to build their own Bloody just the way they like it.

INGREDIENTS

1 pitcher Spicy Bloody Mary mix (see recipe on page 170)

Old Bay seasoning (to rim the glasses)

6 dill pickle spears

½ cup marinated artichoke hearts

½ cup olives stuffed with pimentos, garlic, or blue cheese

⅓ cup pickled mushrooms

⅓ cup Pickled Jalapeños (see recipe on page 141)

⅓ cup giardiniera

⅓ cup roasted red peppers

2 ounces beef jerky

6–8 slices cooked bacon or Candied Bacon (see recipe on page 137)

6–8 pepperoncini peppers

small jar of horseradish

6–8 cooked shrimp

4 ounces cheddar and pepper jack cheese, cubed

6 celery stalks

1 lemon, cut into wedges

1 lime, cut into wedges

toothpicks or skewers

INSTRUCTIONS

1. Make Bloody Mary mix according to recipe instructions. Let sit in refrigerator overnight.

2. Place pitcher or carafe of Bloody Mary mix (alongside your alcohol of choice) next to the board. Place Old Bay–rimmed glasses in the upper corner of the board or next to the board.

3. Put pickles, artichoke hearts, mushrooms, olives, jalapeños, giardiniera, roasted red peppers, beef jerky, bacon, pepperoncini, horseradish, and shrimp into individual small bowls, plates, jars, or other containers (this keeps their flavors and juices separate from each other and allows for a less messy board and easier cleanup)!

4. Arrange the bowls and small plates of garnishes around the board.

5. Fill in gaps on the board with cubed cheese, celery stalks, and lemon and lime wedges.

6. Place toothpicks and skewers on the board or around the board.

7. Let guests build their own Bloody Mary and snacks by selecting their favorite garnishes and adding them directly to their cocktails or toothpicks and skewers.

You can always add additional garnishes or substitute the ones listed for your favorites. Some other great ideas for Bloody Mary garnishes include: mini grilled cheese sandwiches, cheese sticks, meat sticks, fresh or pickled asparagus, pickled okra, oysters, hard boiled eggs, cocktail onions, bell peppers, pepperoni, pickled beets, baby corn, and even a mini cheeseburger slider!

Dessert Board

Prep time: 5 minutes | Active time: 25 minutes | Total time: 30 minutes

My sister, Katie, is the resident baker in our family. Ever since I can remember, she's loved to whip up something sweet in the kitchen. Her cookies, cakes, and crisps are all delicious, but her specialty is definitely pies. And while Katie makes a mean cherry pie and whips up meringue like it's nobody's business, me . . . not so much. I am not a baker.

Which is why I absolutely *love* this dessert platter, because you can satisfy your sweet tooth, no baking required. What *is* required is about ten to fifteen minutes of whipping up a dessert fondue. In this book there are five sweet fondues to choose from (see fondue chapter on page 47). Pair your fondue with fruit like strawberries, bananas, and pineapple, some pre-baked treats like chocolate chip cookies, pound cake, and cheesecake pieces, and something a little salty like pretzels, if you're like me and love a sweet and salty combination, to quickly pull together an easy and pretty dessert. Plus, who doesn't love dipping things in chocolate?

INGREDIENTS

1½ cups (12 ounces) Easy Chocolate Fondue (see recipe on page 63)

16 ounces whole strawberries

2 bananas, sliced

1–2 cups pineapple chunks (about 2 slices per person)

½ pound cake, cubed

1 cup mini pretzel twists

1 cup mini chocolate chip cookies

INSTRUCTIONS

1. Pour chocolate fondue (make according to recipe instructions) into a serving bowl and place in the middle of the board.

2. Arrange the remaining ingredients on board in a circle surrounding the chocolate fondue. If your board is not big enough, arrange some ingredients in a row on another platter (my platter was not large enough to hold everything in a single, circular pattern, so I included the pineapple and pound cake on an additional smaller platter).

3. Serve and enjoy these sweet treats!

There are many other delicious dippers for chocolate fondue that you could include on this dessert platter such as cheesecake bites, donut holes, apples, marshmallows, brownie bites, Rice Krispies Treats, and potato chips.

Fondue Essentials Board

SERVES: 8–10 as an appetizer

Prep time: 20 minutes | Cook time: 20–40 minutes | Active time: 20 minutes | Total time: 60–80 minutes

Cheese fondue is an easy dish to make as an appetizer or full meal. (And make sure you check out my cheese fondue recipes in the next chapter!) Dipping fruits, vegetables, bread, meat, and more in melted cheese creates a fun, interactive experience for your guests while also filling them up. Common dippers like bread and apples are included on this board, along with some more creative options like roasted vegetables and cured meat. Feel free to experiment beyond what's listed here with things like chips, pretzels, Brussels sprouts, carrots, zucchini, shrimp, steak, or ham (the sky's the limit!) because honestly, everything is better dipped in cheese (just make sure whatever you choose to offer will hold together in warm, thick, creamy cheese). If you're choosing food that is normally cooked (like steak, chicken, or vegetables), don't forget to precook before the fun begins.

INGREDIENTS

½ pound potatoes

1 handful asparagus, ends removed

1 cup cauliflower florets

1 cup broccoli florets

1–2 cups mushrooms

2 cups Swiss & Gruyère Fondue (see recipe on page 51)

1 cup cherry tomatoes

2 green apples, sliced

2–3 cups crusty bread, cubed

1 cucumber, sliced

6 ounces salami, sliced

2 bunches grapes

2 bell peppers, sliced

¼ cup cornichons

INSTRUCTIONS

1. Roast the vegetables. Preheat your oven to 400°F and line one or two baking sheets with parchment paper or aluminum foil. Place potatoes, asparagus, broccoli, cauliflower, and mushrooms on baking sheets and drizzle with olive oil and a sprinkling of salt and pepper. Bake until golden brown and tender, 20 to 40 minutes.

2. Pour Swiss and Gruyère fondue (make according to recipe instructions) into a fondue pot, small slow cooker, or bowl. Place on a serving platter or board.

3. Arrange remaining ingredients on serving platter or board around the fondue.

Chapter 3

Fondues

When it comes to melted cheese, I always say "Yes, please!" (Besides dipping things into smooth, creamy, warm cheese, I also love a good rhyme.) Fondues have been gathering people around the table for centuries. Yes, you read that right, centuries; the oldest fondue origin story I could find dates back to the seventeenth century, as a way for Swiss peasants to use winter ingredients like cheese, wine, and bread as they aged. Fondue was popularized in the 1930s by the Swiss Cheese Union, who declared it the official national dish of Switzerland in order to increase cheese consumption (totally here for that!) and made its American debut at the 1964 New York World's Fair, quickly becoming a dinner party staple across the country. So, as a historically essential party platter, fondue really deserves its own chapter in this book.

Think of this as the deliciously warm melty cheese chapter, although there are a few dessert fondues making an appearance too. The warm cheese and chocolate chapter, if you will. And the great thing about fondues, besides melty cheese and warm chocolate, as we've already covered, is that they may seem difficult and time consuming, but they aren't. I promised you approachable, non-intimidating, easy entertaining recipes, and fondues definitely deliver when it comes to both ease and flavor. Many of these recipes come together in just ten to fifteen minutes. A few more tips for your fondue:

- Fondues can be made ahead of time; just keep them warm in a slow cooker or fondue pot until you're ready to serve.

- The standard serving size for cheese fondue is ¼ to ½ cup per person, depending on if you're serving it for an appetizer or a meal. For chocolate or dessert fondue it is about 2 tablespoons to ¼ cup per person.

- Slice and dice a few fruits and vegetables, and please, please, please don't forget plenty of crusty bread (cheese and bread are a match made in heaven) and you've got yourself a party perfect spread that will get people hovering around your table in no time.

Recipe List

Swiss & Gruyère Fondue

SERVES: 8

Prep time: 5 minutes | Cook time: 10–15 minutes | Total time: 15–20 minutes

Traditional Swiss fondue originated in the Alps, so it usually features one or more types of what's called "alpine cheese." Alpine cheese is cheese made in the mountains, using the milk of animals that have grazed in high altitude pastures, which gives the cheese its big, rich, distinct flavor. My spin on traditional Swiss fondue features two of the commonly used alpine cheeses: Emmentaler and Gruyère. These cheeses are shredded, combined with white wine and garlic, and then finished with a pinch of nutmeg to create a deliciously creamy pot of fondue.

INGREDIENTS

1 cup dry white wine

2 cloves garlic, minced

1 teaspoon dry mustard

6 ounces Emmentaler or other Swiss cheese, shredded

6 ounces Gruyère cheese, shredded

2 tablespoons cornstarch

½–1 teaspoon salt, to taste

pinch of nutmeg

crusty bread, tortilla chips, green apples, or vegetables, for serving

INSTRUCTIONS

1. Use a double boiler or heatproof bowl and saucepan to heat up this mixture. Pour a few inches of water into the bottom of your double boiler or a medium saucepan and bring to a boil.

2. Pour white wine in the top portion of the double boiler or in the heatproof bowl (I use a metal mixing bowl). Place over boiling water on top of the saucepan so it nests or balances in the pan and doesn't touch the water.

3. Add minced garlic and mustard powder to the white wine. Whisk to combine.

4. While wine is heating, toss shredded cheese with cornstarch, making sure cheese is fully coated.

5. When the wine mixture is warm (you will know it's ready because the liquid will start to bubble, but do not let it come to a boil), add ⅓ of the cheese and whisk to combine.

6. Once the cheese has been incorporated well and melted, whisk in half of the remaining cheese until smooth.

7. Once that cheese is combined well and melted, add the remaining cheese and whisk until smooth and creamy.

8. Taste the fondue before adding salt. Because cheese can have a naturally salty flavor, you don't want your fondue to be too salty! If you are adding salt, add a little at a time; start with ¼ teaspoon, whisk to combine, then taste the cheese mixture again before gradually adding more salt if needed, ¼ teaspoon at a time.

9. Add pinch of nutmeg. Whisk to combine.

10. Transfer the fondue to a slow cooker or fondue pot to keep warm for serving.

11. Serve with crusty bread, tortilla chips, green apples, and your favorite veggies for dipping!

Beer Cheese Fondue

SERVES: 6–8 as an appetizer, 3–4 as a main

Prep time: 5 minutes | Cook time: 10 minutes | Total time: 15 minutes

Inspired by my favorite football team's fans, known as Cheeseheads, this fondue combines sharp cheddar cheese and light beer to make a smooth and creamy beer cheese dip in just fifteen minutes. I like to melt everything together on the stove before my guests arrive and then transfer it to a small slow cooker or fondue pot so I won't miss out on some ooey gooey cheese dipping action!

INGREDIENTS

8 ounces beer (I recommend light lager, Saison, or IPA for a hoppy flavor)

3 cloves garlic, minced (or 1 teaspoon garlic powder)

2 teaspoons dry mustard

2 teaspoons Worcestershire sauce

2½–3 cups (10–12 ounces) sharp cheddar cheese, shredded

2 tablespoons flour or cornstarch

crusty bread, tortilla chips, green apples, or vegetables, for serving

INSTRUCTIONS

1. Use a double boiler or heatproof bowl and saucepan to heat up this mixture. Pour a few inches of water into the bottom of your double boiler or a saucepan and bring to a boil.

2. Combine beer, garlic, dry mustard, and Worcestershire in the top portion of the double boiler or in the heatproof bowl (I use a metal mixing bowl). Place over boiling water on top of the saucepan so it nests or balances in the pan and doesn't touch the water. Whisk to combine.

3. Toss shredded cheese with flour or cornstarch, making sure flour coats all of the shredded cheese.

4. When the beer mixture is warm (you will know it's ready because the liquid will start to bubble), add ⅓ of the cheese and whisk to combine.

5. Once the cheese has been incorporated well and melted, whisk in half of the remaining cheese until smooth.

6. Once that cheese is combined well and melted, add the remaining cheese and whisk until smooth and creamy. Add 2½ cups cheese for a thinner fondue, and 3 cups of cheese for a thicker, creamier fondue.

7. Transfer the beer cheese fondue to a slow cooker or fondue pot to keep warm for serving.

8. Serve with crusty bread, tortilla chips, green apples, and your favorite veggies for dipping!

If the beer mixture is not warm before you start adding the cheese, there is a chance the fondue will separate, leaving you with an orange liquid and a clump of melted cheese. If you have a fondue pot, you can complete all steps in a fondue pot. Wait until beer mixture is warm and then gradually add the cheese to the fondue pot.

Bourbon Gouda Fondue

SERVES: 4

Prep time: 5 minutes | Cook time: 10–15 minutes | Total time: 15–20 minutes

AJ and I have been indulging in Beer Cheese Fondue (see recipe on page 52) on game days for years. One fall Sunday while I was whipping us up a batch before kickoff, I got to thinking, if we can make fondue with wine or beer, why not with bourbon too? After doing a little research on flavors and pairings, I learned that while a variety of different cheeses pair well with bourbon (and it made me want to host a bourbon and cheese tasting party at our house!), aged Gouda cheese may be the ultimate cheese for pairing with bourbon. Aged Gouda's creamy and smoky notes complement bourbon's smooth, oaky, and spicy essence without washing out either's flavor. From there, I shredded some Gouda, added a little wine to balance the fondue and not overpower our palates with a powerful bourbon punch, and got to heating and dipping.

INGREDIENTS

½ cup dry white wine

2 ounces bourbon

½ pound aged Gouda cheese, shredded

2 tablespoons cornstarch

½ teaspoon salt

crusty bread, tortilla chips, green apples, or vegetables, for serving

INSTRUCTIONS

1. Use a double boiler or heatproof bowl and saucepan to heat up this mixture. Pour a few inches of water into the bottom of your double boiler or a medium saucepan and bring to a boil.

2. Pour white wine and bourbon in the top portion of the double boiler or in the heatproof bowl (I use a metal mixing bowl). Place over boiling water on top of the saucepan or pot so it nests or balances in the pan/pot and doesn't touch the water. Whisk to combine.

3. While wine and bourbon are heating, toss shredded Gouda cheese with cornstarch, making sure cheese is fully coated.

4. When the wine and bourbon mixture is warm (you will know it's ready because the liquid will start to bubble, but do not let it come to a boil), add ⅓ of the cheese and whisk to combine.

5. Once the cheese has been incorporated well and melted, whisk in half of the remaining cheese until smooth.

6. Once that cheese is combined well and melted, add the remaining cheese and whisk until smooth and creamy.

7. Season with salt. Whisk to combine. Taste the cheese mixture and gradually add more salt if needed.

8. Transfer the fondue to a slow cooker or fondue pot to keep warm for serving.

9. Serve with crusty bread, tortilla chips, green apples, and your favorite veggies for dipping.

Baked Fondue with Red Wine & Caramelized Onions

SERVES: 6–8

Prep time: 10 minutes | Cook time: 45–60 minutes | Total time: 55–70 minutes

I love the Food Network. One of the best tips I ever got from a Food Network show that I've carried with me in my own cooking over the years is "brown food tastes good." This mantra is the key to this caramelized onion fondue; you want to get your onions to a beautiful brownish bronze color and a soft, jammy texture. The other key to delicious deep flavors for this fondue is patience; allow the onions to cook slowly over low heat on the stove for as long as they need (sometimes, depending on your own stove, more than thirty minutes). This process allows the onions to slowly release their natural sugars, caramelize, and develop flavor. While this caramelization process takes time and a whole lot of patience, the payoff will be extremely rewarding, creating a fondue with layers of flavor, giving it a French onion soup vibe. I promise you'll taste the payoff for your patience with the first bite.

INGREDIENTS

2 tablespoons butter

2 medium red onions, thinly sliced

1½ teaspoons salt, divided

½ cup dry red wine

8 ounces cream cheese, softened to room temperature

1½ cups shredded Gruyère cheese, divided

1 teaspoon dried thyme

¼ cup Parmesan cheese, shredded

crusty bread, pita chips, or tortilla chips, for serving

INSTRUCTIONS

1. Caramelize onions. Heat butter in a large pan or skillet over medium heat until melted and bubbling. Gradually add sliced onions and cook, stirring occasionally, until onions are soft. Season onions with some of the salt. Repeat until all onion slices have been added. Reduce heat to medium low or low and cook, stirring occasionally, for about 30 to 40 minutes until onions are super soft and caramelized. They should turn a medium brown color but should not be crispy or burned.

2. Deglaze the pan with red wine. Pour wine into the pan with the onions. Stir into the onions, scraping up any browned bits from the pan. Let liquid bubble and evaporate, then remove pan from the heat when the liquid has reduced but is not completely evaporated from the pan (reduce by at least half if not a little more than that).

3. Preheat oven to 400°F and lightly spray an ovenproof baking dish with cooking spray.

4. Combine onion and wine mixture, cream cheese, 1 cup of the Gruyère, remaining salt, and thyme in a mixing bowl. Using a wooden spoon, stir to combine. Once combined, pour onion and cheese mixture into the baking dish. Top with the remaining Gruyère as well as the Parmesan cheese.

5. Bake in the oven for about 20 minutes, until cheese is melted and bubbly. Keep the baked fondue in the oven and switch the oven to your broil setting. Keeping a close eye on the fondue so it does not burn, broil for about 3 to 5 minutes until cheese is browned.

6. Serve immediately with crusty bread, pita chips, or tortilla chips for dipping.

Loaded Potato Fondue

SERVES: 6–8

Prep time: 5 minutes | Cook time: 20–25 minutes | Total time: 25–30 minutes

Growing up, my mom's twice baked potatoes were one of my favorite dinners. We usually ate the potatoes, which had been cooked, scooped out, mixed with butter and cheese, and then baked again alongside a juicy piece of grilled steak, another one of my favorites. My dad always loved to top his with a dollop of sour cream, and it was an extra special treat when some leftover bacon was chopped up and thrown into the mix. This fondue takes all the flavors of one of my favorite comfort foods and turns them into a party worthy appetizer. Potatoes are the obvious dipper of choice for this fondue, but other vegetables, bread, and crackers would also be delicious.

INGREDIENTS

6 slices bacon

1 cup vegetable broth

2 cloves garlic, minced

½ teaspoon Worcestershire sauce

8 ounces Gruyère cheese, shredded

4 ounces sharp cheddar cheese, shredded

2 tablespoons cornstarch

¼ cup sour cream

½ to 1 teaspoon salt, more to taste

½ teaspoon pepper, more to taste

2 tablespoons fresh chives or green onions, minced

boiled or roasted potatoes and/ or vegetables, for serving

INSTRUCTIONS

1. Cook the bacon. Heat a medium pan over medium heat. Cook bacon until brown and crispy, about 5 to 8 minutes. Set aside to cool. Once cool enough to handle, dice.

2. Use a double boiler or heatproof bowl and saucepan to heat up this mixture. Pour a few inches of water into the bottom of your double boiler or saucepan and bring to a boil.

3. Pour vegetable broth into the top portion of the double boiler or in the heatproof bowl (I use a metal mixing bowl). Place over boiling water on top of the saucepan or pot so it nests or balances in the pan/pot and doesn't touch the water.

4. Add minced garlic and Worcestershire sauce to the vegetable broth. Whisk to combine.

5. While broth is heating, toss the shredded Gruyère and cheddar cheeses with cornstarch, making sure cheeses are fully coated.

6. When broth is warm (you will know it's ready because the liquid will start to bubble, but do not let it come to a boil), add ⅓ of the cheese and whisk to combine. Once the cheese has been incorporated well and melted, whisk in half of the remaining cheese until smooth. Once that cheese is combined well and melted, add the remaining cheese and whisk until smooth and creamy.

7. Mix in sour cream and half of the bacon. Season with salt and pepper. Whisk to combine. Taste the cheese mixture and gradually add more salt and pepper if needed or desired.

8. Transfer the fondue to a slow cooker or fondue pot to keep warm for serving. Top with minced chives or scallions and remaining bacon. Serve with potatoes and/or other veggies for dipping.

Chile con Queso

SERVES: 8

Prep time: 10 minutes | Cook time: 15 minutes | Total time: 25 minutes

This easy at-home Tex-Mex version of "fondue" (we've got melted cheese with a spicy spin so it totally qualifies!) comes together on your stovetop in just one saucepan and in less than thirty minutes. It's so creamy and irresistible that when it's ready, we hover around the stove just waiting to dip our first chips!

INGREDIENTS

2 tablespoons butter

½ red onion, minced

1 fresh jalapeño or 1 heaping tablespoon Pickled Jalapeños (see recipe on page 141), minced (optional, omit if you don't like spicy food)

2 cloves garlic, minced

¼ teaspoon cumin

½ teaspoon salt

8 ounces white American cheese, diced

8 ounces pepper jack cheese, diced

½ cup half-and-half

dash of nutmeg

1 (10-ounce) can diced tomatoes and green chilies, drained

tortilla chips, for serving

I recommend buying cheese from the deli counter and then dicing it into smaller pieces, rather than buying pre cubed or pre-shredded cheese. It will result in a creamier queso texture.

INSTRUCTIONS

1. Heat a large saucepan, Dutch oven, or deep skillet over medium heat and add butter. Once butter is melted, add onion, jalapeño (if using), garlic, cumin, and salt and sauté for 4 to 5 minutes until vegetables are soft and onions are translucent, but haven't developed much color.

2. Add diced cheese a little a time (start by adding the American cheese because it melts faster) and whisk to combine. As cheese starts to melt, add more cheese a handful at a time. Stir continuously so the cheese doesn't burn at the bottom of the pan. Once you've added all the cheese, reduce the heat to medium low and add about half (¼ cup) of the half-and-half and whisk to combine.

3. Whisk the cheese and milk mixture until creamy and smooth. Simmer the queso over low heat for about 10 minutes, stirring often. While the queso is simmering, gradually add the remaining half-and-half a little at a time until you reach your desired thickness and consistency.

4. Add dash of nutmeg, stir to combine.

5. Remove pan from heat, add in ½ can of the diced tomatoes and green chilies. Evaluate consistency of the queso and add in the remaining ½ can of diced tomatoes and chilies if you prefer a chunkier dip.

6. Transfer queso to a bowl and serve warm as a component on the Elevate Your Tailgate Board (see recipe on page 26) or as a dip trio with the Chunky Habanero Salsa (see recipe on page 80) and Super Simple Guacamole (see recipe on page 79). Make sure you have lots of tortilla chips for dipping!

7. To keep queso warm for an extended period of time, transfer it to a fondue pot or small slow cooker set to the "warm" or lowest setting. To reheat, add queso to a small saucepan and reheat over medium low heat stirring consistently until warm. You can also reheat in a microwave safe bowl in 30-second intervals, stirring in between. You may need to add a few tablespoons of half-and-half when reheating if queso is too thick.

Easy Chocolate Fondue

SERVES: 6–8

Cook time: 8–10 minutes | Total time: 8–10 minutes

Chocolate fondue is a rich, creamy, decadent dessert that you can make in less than ten minutes. Serve it with an assortment of fruits, sweets like pound cake, cheesecake, cookies, brownies, and even some salty snacks, like pretzels and potato chips, and you have the perfect sweet treat for a quiet, romantic date night at home or the finale of a dinner party.

INGREDIENTS

½ cup half-and-half

1 cup dark chocolate chips

½ cup milk chocolate chips

½ teaspoon vanilla

sea salt, to taste

fruit or other sweet treats of choice, for serving

Substitute orange extract, almond extract, or peppermint extract for the vanilla extract to create different flavors depending on the season!

INSTRUCTIONS

1. Use a double boiler or heatproof bowl to heat up this mixture. Pour a few inches of water into the bottom of your double boiler or a medium saucepan and bring to a boil.

2. Place the heatproof (I use metal) bowl on top of the saucepan or pot so it nests or balances in the pan/pot and doesn't touch the water.

3. Add half-and-half to bowl or double boiler.

4. Once half-and-half is warmed (5 minutes), gradually add the chocolate chips, about ½ cup at a time. Whisk consistently as you add the chocolate, waiting to add more chocolate until the chocolate has melted and smoothly incorporated into the half-and-half.

5. Once all chocolate is added and melted, whisk until smooth.

6. Remove from heat and whisk in vanilla.

7. Transfer to small fondue pot, small crock pot, or small bowl to serve. Add sea salt to taste on top.

8. Serve with a variety of fruit or other sweet dippers.

Leftover Halloween Candy Fondue

SERVES: 8–10

Active time: 5 minutes | Cook time: 2 hours | Total time: 2 hours, 5 minutes

As kids, my sister and I would take pillowcases trick or treating to really maximize our Halloween haul as we canvassed every single house in our neighborhood. After weeks of mom-ordered candy rationing, and even with some sneaky candy stealers living in our house (Mom and Dad, I know what you were up to) we still had candy littering our kitchen cabinets that would inevitably go to waste, so the idea for this fondue came from thinking about all of those poor, sad, fun sized leftovers. Why not put them to good use, throw them all in a slow cooker with a little cream, and melt them until they're smooth and creamy? This would be such a fun and festive recipe for a Halloween party (no need to wait for the leftovers to make it!) or a creative way to use the chocolate that goes on sale just after Valentine's Day or Easter.

INGREDIENTS

12 miniature peanut butter cups

15 miniature or snack size candy bars

½ cup M&Ms

½ cup semi-sweet chocolate chips

½ cup half-and-half

fruit, cookies, brownies, cake, or pretzels, for serving

INSTRUCTIONS

1. Unwrap all individually wrapped candies.

2. Add all ingredients to a slow cooker.

3. Cook on low for 1½ to 2 hours, stirring occasionally, until the fondue is creamy and smooth.

4. Serve with fruit, cookies, brownies, cake, pretzels, or other dippers, or as a part of the Dessert Board (see recipe on page 42).

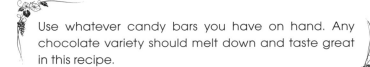

Use whatever candy bars you have on hand. Any chocolate variety should melt down and taste great in this recipe.

Cheesecake Fondue

SERVES: 8–10

Cook time: 10–15 minutes | Total time: 10–15 minutes

My lack of baking skills, plus my love for a delicious slice of creamy cheesecake, inspired this recipe for Cheesecake Fondue. Combine cream, white chocolate, cream cheese, lemon juice, vanilla, and a little bit of cinnamon to get a cheesecake flavor without even thinking about a water bath. The key to getting this cheesecake fondue perfectly smooth and creamy is cubing room temperature cream cheese and adding it a little at a time until its completely incorporated and melted into the cream and white chocolate. Sign me up for a dessert that combines all of the flavors of a good piece of cheesecake in less than half the time into a thick, creamy dip perfect for anything from fresh fruit to graham crackers or even brownie bites. I'm drooling just thinking about it.

INGREDIENTS

⅓ cup half-and-half

11 ounces (about 2 cups) white chocolate chips

8 ounces cream cheese, cubed and softened to room temperature

½ teaspoon vanilla extract

juice of ½ lemon (about 1 tablespoon fresh lemon juice)

¼ teaspoon cinnamon

fruit or other sweet treats of choice, for serving

INSTRUCTIONS

1. Use a double boiler or heatproof bowl to heat up this mixture. Pour a few inches of water into the bottom of your double boiler or a medium saucepan and bring to a boil.

2. Place a heatproof (I use metal) bowl on top of the saucepan so it nests or balances in the pan and doesn't touch the water.

3. Add half-and-half to bowl or double boiler.

4. Once half-and-half is warmed (5 minutes), gradually add the white chocolate chips, about ½ cup at a time. Whisk consistently as you add the chocolate, waiting to add more chocolate until the chocolate has melted and smoothly incorporated into the half-and-half.

5. Once all chocolate is added and melted, whisk until smooth.

6. Gradually add the cream cheese a few cubes at a time. Whisk consistently as you add the cream cheese, waiting to add more cream cheese until it is melted and smoothly incorporated.

7. Remove from heat and whisk in vanilla, lemon juice, and cinnamon.

8. Transfer to small fondue pot, small slow cooker, or small bowl to serve.

9. Serve with a variety of fruit or other sweet dippers.

S'mores Fondue

SERVES: 6–8

Cook time: 10 minutes | Total time: 10 minutes

No campfire needed! A nod to everyone's favorite summertime dessert (and one of my favorite movies, *The Sandlot*), this fondue gives you all the ooey gooey goodness of toasted marshmallows anytime you want it with just a few minutes in your oven. Featuring smooth, melted chocolate combined with marshmallow fluff, topped with campfire marshmallows broiled until bubbly and a toasty, golden brown, this delicious fondue delivers s'mores flavors sans campfires, and honestly, the mess that comes with it. Don't forget the graham crackers for dipping.

INGREDIENTS

½ cup half-and-half

1½ cups chocolate chips (I used a combination of milk and semi-sweet chocolate)

2 tablespoons marshmallow fluff

15 whole marshmallows

graham crackers and fruit, for serving

INSTRUCTIONS

1. Use a double boiler or heatproof bowl to heat up this mixture. Pour a few inches of water into the bottom of your double boiler or a medium saucepan and bring to a boil.

2. Place a heatproof (I use metal) bowl on top of the saucepan so it nests or balances in the pan and doesn't touch the water.

3. Add half-and-half to bowl or double boiler.

4. Once half-and-half is warmed (5 minutes), gradually add the chocolate chips, about ½ cup at a time. Whisk consistently as you add the chocolate, waiting to add more chocolate until the chocolate has melted and smoothly incorporated into the half-and-half.

5. Once all chocolate is added and melted, whisk until smooth.

6. Add marshmallow fluff. Whisk until combined and smooth.

7. Remove from heat and pour melted chocolate mixture into an ovenproof skillet or baking dish. Gently place marshmallows on top of chocolate in a circular pattern.

8. Preheat your oven to broil.

9. Place skillet or baking dish on upper oven rack under the broiler. Broil until marshmallows are browned, about 2 to 3 minutes. Keep a close watch on the marshmallows so they don't burn.

10. Serve with graham crackers and fruit for dipping.

Turtle Fondue

SERVES: 6–8

Cook time: 15 minutes | Total time: 15 minutes

The word turtle is often used to describe the flavor combination of chocolate, caramel, and pecans. It's not because the original pecan and caramel candies, which are then dipped in chocolate, contain any parts of a turtle. Instead, the name comes from a salesman in the early 1900s who thought the small chocolate shapes resembled tiny turtles. Similarly, this sweet fondue doesn't contain any turtle parts, but is a creamy and crunchy combination of the classic "turtle" flavors: caramel, pecans, and chocolate.

INGREDIENTS

¼ cup half-and-half

15 caramel candies, unwrapped

½ cup half-and-half

1 cup dark chocolate chips

½ cup milk chocolate chips

⅓ cup whole or chopped pecans

fruit or other sweet treats of choice, for serving

Melting caramel candies was an easier way to achieve my desired result and consistency rather than making caramel from scratch but you can use homemade caramel sauce (by combining cream and sugar) or store-bought caramel sauce (the caramel ice cream topping that comes in a jar has the right consistency) in this recipe.

INSTRUCTIONS

1. Use a double boiler or heatproof bowl to heat up this mixture. Pour a few inches of water into the bottom of your double boiler or a medium saucepan and bring to a boil.

2. Place a heatproof (I use metal) bowl on top of the saucepan so it nests or balances in the pan and doesn't touch the water.

3. Add ¼ cup half-and-half to bowl or double boiler.

4. Once half-and-half is warmed (5 minutes), gradually add the unwrapped caramel candies, whisking to combine.

5. Once half-and-half is melted and smooth, transfer caramel sauce to a bowl and set aside.

6. In the same metal bowl, add ½ cup half-and-half.

7. Once caramel is warmed, add the chocolate chips, about ½ cup at a time. Whisk consistently as you add the chocolate, waiting to add more chocolate until the chocolate has melted and smoothly incorporated into the half-and-half.

8. Once all chocolate is added and melted, whisk until smooth.

9. Add caramel sauce to the chocolate, whisk until smooth.

10. Add pecans to the chocolate and caramel. Whisk until combined.

11. Transfer to small fondue pot, small crock pot, or small bowl to serve. Add additional pecans to top as desired.

12. Serve with a variety of fruit or other sweet dippers.

Chapter 4

Dips & Spreads

Growing up, I always loved helping my mom in the kitchen. I remember my first actual job helping (rather than just doing my homework at the kitchen table while she cooked dinner) was making dips and sauces that accompanied our meal, like guacamole on taco night or the cranberry sauce on Thanksgiving. This chapter is dedicated to the recipes for slathering, spreading, dipping, and dunking that gave me my start in the kitchen. Make familiar classics like Super Simple Guacamole (see recipe on page 79), Chunky Habanero Salsa (see recipe on page 80), Fresh Basil Pesto (see recipe on page 92), or Herb Cream Cheese (see recipe on page 91) with fresh ingredients. Or, discover new flavors and favorites, like Roasted Beet Dip (see recipe on page 95), Curried White Bean Dip (see recipe on page 96), or Bee Sting Chèvre Spread (see recipe on page 83). Here's to scooping and sharing. Chips, ahoy!

Recipe List

Pimento Cheese

SERVES: 12–14

Prep time: 5 minutes | Active time: 10 minutes | Total time: 15 minutes

Pimento cheese may be the South's favorite spread, and for good reason. How could anyone not love a delicious, creamy combination of cream cheese, cheddar cheese, pimento peppers, and mayo (for a little extra binding and flavor, of course)? This Southern staple makes appearances everywhere, from picnics to potlucks, and even makes the menu in some fine dining restaurants. This recipe can be used in a wide variety of ways: as a dip, in sandwiches and on top of burgers, mixed in with loaded French fries or nachos, as a way to enhance deviled eggs (see my Pimento Cheese Deviled Egg recipe on page 110), and even in baked goods like muffins and scones. This interpretation of the popular classic is sure to be a hit no matter the occasion.

INGREDIENTS

1 (8-ounce) block sharp white cheddar cheese, shredded

1 (8-ounce) block sharp orange cheddar cheese, shredded

8 ounces cream cheese, softened at room temperature and cubed

1 (7-ounce) jar pimentos, drained

½ cup mayonnaise

1 teaspoon garlic powder

1 teaspoon onion powder

½–1 teaspoon crushed red pepper flakes

2 tablespoons pickle juice or olive juice

salt and pepper, to taste

¼ cup Pickled Jalapeños (see recipe on page 141), diced, (optional)

INSTRUCTIONS

1. Using a box grater, shred both kinds of cheddar cheese. (Don't use pre-shredded, bagged cheese for this recipe. Shredding higher quality cheddar by hand is worth it.)

2. Add all ingredients, except salt and pepper, to the bowl of a stand mixer or a large mixing bowl.

3. Beat the mixture together using a stand mixer or handheld mixer on low, or by hand using a large, sturdy wooden spoon or spatula until well combined.

4. Taste pimento cheese, add a few turns or shakes of salt and black pepper, and mix again to combine.

5. Serve pimento cheese immediately with crackers or pretzels, as a component on the Elevate Your Tailgate Board (see recipe on page 26), or the Ultimate Cheddar Snack Board (see recipe on page 14), or use to make Pimento Cheese Deviled Eggs (see recipe on page 110).

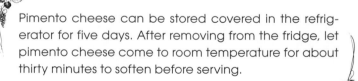

Pimento cheese can be stored covered in the refrigerator for five days. After removing from the fridge, let pimento cheese come to room temperature for about thirty minutes to soften before serving.

Roasted Garlic Dip

SERVES: 6–8

Prep time: 5 minutes | Cook time: 40 minutes | Active time: 5 minutes | Total time: 50 minutes

You know those totally addicting chip dips that make you want to continually hover near the snack table at parties? This Roasted Garlic Dip is quickly going to become a staple on your snack table! Simple, delicious ingredients shine in this super easy, one-bowl recipe. Creamy sour cream (or non-fat Greek yogurt for a more calorie conscious, tangier option), fresh thyme and rosemary, nutty Parmesan cheese, bright lemon juice, and lots of soft, caramelized garlic come together to make a totally craveable, addictive spread that's perfect for dipping everything from fresh or grilled vegetables, chips, or sliced bread!

INGREDIENTS

3 heads garlic

olive oil

8 ounces sour cream or non-fat Greek yogurt

1 teaspoon fresh thyme leaves, removed from stem and roughly chopped

1 teaspoon fresh rosemary leaves, removed from stem and roughly chopped

1 tablespoon lemon juice

⅓ cup Parmesan cheese, shredded

salt and pepper, to taste

pinch of cayenne pepper, if desired

grilled veggies, grilled or sliced bread, pretzels, potato chips, or crackers, for serving

INSTRUCTIONS

1. Preheat your oven to 400°F.

2. Prep garlic. With a sharp knife, slice the top of the head of garlic to expose all cloves. Place each head of garlic on a separate sheet of aluminum foil and drizzle exposed cloves with olive oil. Wrap each garlic head in foil and roast in the oven for 40 minutes until cloves are golden brown and soft. Once garlic is cooled, it should be really easy to squeeze the soft cloves out of the garlic heads. Squeeze all garlic into a medium bowl and mash with a fork into a paste.

3. In the same bowl, add sour cream or Greek yogurt, thyme, rosemary, and lemon juice. Stir well to combine.

4. Add shredded Parmesan into bowl with the garlic dip. Stir well to combine.

5. Finish with salt and pepper to taste. Add a pinch of cayenne pepper to add heat if desired.

6. Serve with your favorite grilled veggies (Roasted Garlic Dip is an essential component to the Summer Grilled Fruit & Veggie Board, see recipe on page 21), crudités (it would make a great addition to the Colorful Crudités Platter, see recipe on page 30), grilled or sliced bread, pretzels, potato chips, or crackers.

Greek yogurt has a similar creamy texture and consistency to sour cream, but has a slightly different and stronger flavor, which will affect the flavor of this dip (AJ and I both preferred the sour cream version). I wanted to include both versions in case you were looking for an easy way to serve a lightened-up version of this dip, in which case you should opt for Greek yogurt over sour cream.

Super Simple Guacamole

SERVES: 8–10

Prep time: 5 minutes | Active time: 5 minutes | Total time: 10 minutes

Guacamole was one of the first things I learned how to make. Taco night was on the regular weeknight dinner rotation in our house, and for as long as I can remember I'd help my mom whip up a quick guac, which means I've been a guacamole maker since elementary school. This guac is a little different than the one I made for family taco nights, but that's because I've had twenty or so years to perfect my guacamole making craft. This recipe delivers the perfect balance of everything you want in a great guacamole: the right amount of creaminess from ripe avocados; the right amount of texture from chunky tomatoes and diced onions; the right amount of tanginess from lemon juice; the right amount of herbiness (not a word but I'm making it one!) from fresh cilantro; and the right amount of spice from jalapeños. This guac is so good that usually I don't have time to transfer it to a serving bowl before we start dipping chips into the mixing bowl that I made it in.

INGREDIENTS

3 ripe avocados

½ medium red onion, diced

½ large tomato or 1 Roma tomato, diced

1 jalapeño, diced, seeds removed (or if you like your guac a little spicy, keep some of the jalapeño seeds and add them in!)

1½ teaspoons garlic powder

2 tablespoons lemon juice (juice of one lemon or a little more)

1 bunch cilantro (about 2 tablespoons)

salt, to taste

tortilla chips, for serving

INSTRUCTIONS

1. Slice avocados in half. Remove pits and scoop avocado flesh into a large bowl.

2. Mash avocados with a potato masher or the back of a fork until they reach your desired consistency. (I like my guacamole a little chunky while others prefer theirs super smooth.) The avocados will get a little softer as you add other ingredients and mix them in, so be careful not to over mash.

3. Add diced onion, tomato, and jalapeño into the bowl. Stir to combine.

4. Add garlic powder to avocado mixture and stir to combine.

5. Gradually add lemon juice (squeeze in a little at a time and stir to check the consistency to make sure you haven't added too much) and stir to combine. Make sure you don't add too much or you'll end up with soupy guac.

6. Finish off with cilantro and a pinch of salt.

7. Serve with crispy tortilla chips for maximum dipping!

You can substitute lime juice for lemon juice.

Chunky Habanero Salsa

SERVES: 5–6

Active time: 20 minutes | Additional time: 30 minutes | Total time: 50 minutes

I am not the resident salsa creator in our house. My husband, AJ, is, so this book features one exclusive recipe created and made by AJ—and I know you're going to love it. AJ gets his salsa making abilities from his dad, who makes fresh batches of this addicting dip with tomatoes and peppers from his garden all summer long, so I immediately had AJ call his dad for his ingredient list and start his salsa testing. We dipped many, many chips to make sure the spice and seasoning was perfect. (Salsa taste testing is hard y'all but someone's got to do it.) If you've never worked with habaneros before, don't be intimidated. Yes, they are spicy, but I love the heat level and slow burn they give to this salsa. Just start with a small amount and then taste to see if you need more heat. And if you can't find habaneros or are still a little nervous, that's okay! Substitute a few jalapeños instead.

INGREDIENTS

4–5 (4 cups) medium ripe tomatoes, diced

½ (1 cup) large white onion, diced

1 cup cilantro, removed from stems and coarsely chopped

2 habanero or jalapeño peppers, finely chopped

8 ounces tomato sauce

½ teaspoon white pepper or more to taste

¼ teaspoon salt or more to taste

tortilla chips, for serving

INSTRUCTIONS

1. Combine all ingredients except for tortilla chips in a large bowl and stir together until well combined.

2. Cover and refrigerate salsa for at least 30 minutes or longer before serving. This rest time will allow the ingredients to, in AJ's words, "mesh better" and create a deeper, spicier, more complex flavor.

3. Add additional salt and pepper as needed to taste before serving.

4. Serve with tortilla chips for dipping or as part of a dip trio with Chile con Queso (see recipe page on page 60) and Super Simple Guacamole (see recipe on page 79).

Habanero peppers pack a punch when it comes to heat and flavor, much more than the more common jalapeño pepper. Habaneros are anywhere from twelve to one hundred times hotter than a jalapeño, so when you're chopping them, handle them with caution and care. This includes wearing plastic gloves to protect your fingers, and not touching your eyes after chopping the peppers.

Bee Sting Chèvre Spread

SERVES: 4

Total time: 5 minutes

I could wax poetic about this Bee Sting Chèvre Spread, or I could simply just get to the point. I am a huge sucker for anything that's a little sweet and a little spicy. Goat cheese and honey is a sweet, creamy, classic combination, so this simple spread adds a little kick to the classic with a sprinkling of cayenne and a dash of thyme. And that's it. Just a short little introduction for a four-ingredient dip that really needs no introduction other than delicious food doesn't have to be complicated or fussy.

INGREDIENTS

4 ounces chèvre or goat cheese

3 teaspoons honey

¼ teaspoon cayenne pepper

¼ teaspoon dried thyme

sliced bread, crackers, or
   veggies, for serving

INSTRUCTIONS

1. In a small bowl, combine cheese, honey, and spices. Stir well to incorporate and infuse flavors into the cheese.

2. Serve as a component of the Summer Grilled Fruit & Veggie Board (see recipe on page 21) or the Colorful Crudités Platter (see recipe on page 30), or as a standalone spread or dip for sliced bread, crackers, or your favorite vegetables.

Grilled Brie with Blackberry Balsamic Glaze

SERVES: 8

Prep time: 5 minutes | Cook time: 10 minutes | Total time: 15 minutes

My dad (who is not much of a cook . . . his kitchen repertoire is limited to omelets, sandwiches, and ordering pizza) makes a mean grilled cheese. While this recipe has little in common with my dad's classic grilled cheese sandwiches (sliced cheddar on wheat), they do share a name, so whenever I think about this recipe, I'm immediately transported back to weekend lunches and dinners when Dad was in charge of the menu. The grilled cheese we're talking about here is a regular in our appetizer recipe rotation, especially in the summertime, when the last thing we want to do is preheat the oven. Grilled Brie is the oven-free alternative to the well-known cocktail and holiday party mainstay baked Brie (see Cranberry-Walnut Baked Brie recipe on page 87). And because I equate grilling with summer, I put a warm-weather spin on this recipe with fresh blackberries and basil (but any other berry works too, so pick your favorite)! I love how quickly this easy, elevated appetizer comes together almost as much as I love grilled cheese.

INGREDIENTS

¼ cup balsamic vinegar

2 tablespoons brown sugar

1 tablespoon honey

1 tablespoon lemon juice

1 cup blackberries

1 bunch basil, julienned

8-ounce wheel Brie

1 teaspoon olive oil

baguette or crackers, for serving

INSTRUCTIONS

1. Combine vinegar, brown sugar, honey, and lemon juice in a small saucepan and bring to a boil.

2. Reduce heat to low and simmer for about ten minutes until thick and syrupy (the balsamic mixture should easily coat the back of a spoon).

3. Remove from heat and let cool.

4. Mix blackberries and basil into the balsamic glaze. Set aside.

5. Preheat grill to medium high.

6. Brush Brie cheese rind with olive oil on each side and place on hot grill.

7. Grill Brie about two minutes per side, until cheese is soft and warm and grill marks are visible.

8. Transfer cheese to a serving plate or platter and top with blackberry balsamic mixture.

9. Serve as a component of the UnBrielievable Board (see recipe on page 17) or the Summer Grilled Fruit & Veggie Board (see recipe on page 21). Brie goes great with veggies! Make sure you also have plenty of baguette or your favorite crackers on hand for epic cheese pulls and lots of dipping.

Strawberries, blueberries, or raspberries can be used in lieu of blackberries.

Cranberry-Walnut Baked Brie

SERVES: 8

Prep time: 5 minutes | Cook time: 15 minutes | Total time: 20 minutes

Some of the best appetizer recipes are the easiest. Like this baked Brie, a take on the popular staple on many a holiday party menu that features creamy cheese and crisp puff pastry. What I love about this rich and luxurious appetizer, besides the creamy cheese and warm winter flavors, is that it takes little effort but delivers a big payout. I guarantee your guests will gather around it, excitedly scooping up bits of Brie, cranberries, walnuts, and honey on pieces of bread, crackers, and apples until there's nothing left.

INGREDIENTS

½ cup walnuts

8-ounce wheel Brie

¼ cup honey

1 tablespoon water

¼ teaspoon nutmeg

¼–½ cup dried cranberries

2 sprigs rosemary leaves, removed from stems

crackers, apples, or crusty bread, for serving

INSTRUCTIONS

1. Preheat your oven to 350°F.

2. Toast walnuts on a baking sheet for 5 to 10 minutes until golden brown and fragrant.

3. While the walnuts are toasting, remove the top rind of the Brie round, leaving about ½-inch border from the edge of the Brie. The easiest way to remove the top rind is to use a knife to score around the top of the Brie and then use a spoon to scrape and remove it.

4. Place Brie in an ovenproof baking dish, a cast iron skillet, or on a baking sheet with parchment paper and bake for 12 to 15 minutes until soft (but not runny).

5. While the Brie is baking, make your topping. In a saucepan over medium low heat add honey, water, and nutmeg. Stir to combine and cook over low heat until honey starts to bubble.

6. Stir in cranberries, walnuts, and rosemary. Reduce heat to low to keep mixture warm, stirring occasionally.

7. Once Brie is soft, take out of oven and top with cranberry-walnut mixture.

8. Serve while warm with crackers, apples, and crusty bread.

You can substitute your favorite nuts for the walnuts. Pecans and almonds would both taste great!

Smoked Salmon Spread

SERVES: 8–10

Active time: 10 minutes

While commonly associated with breakfast or brunch, smoked salmon can be served any time of day. This creamy spread is of course delicious slathered on a toasted bagel, but also makes a quick, easy, and flavorful appetizer with crackers or cucumber slices.

INGREDIENTS

8 ounces cream cheese, softened to room temperature

2 tablespoons half-and-half

3 teaspoons lemon juice

1 teaspoon Worcestershire sauce

1 teaspoon dried chives

3 tablespoons capers, drained

¼ teaspoon salt

¼ teaspoon pepper

1 cup smoked salmon, roughly chopped

bagels, toasted bread, pita chips, or sliced vegetables, for serving

INSTRUCTIONS

1. Add cream cheese and half-and-half to the bowl of a stand mixer or a mixing bowl.

2. Using a stand mixer or hand mixer with a whisk attachment, mix cream cheese and half-and-half for about 2 minutes until lightly whipped.

3. Add lemon juice, Worcestershire sauce, chives, capers, salt, and pepper to the whipped cream cheese and mix for another 1 to 2 minutes until incorporated, but not overwhipped.

4. Add roughly chopped smoked salmon to whipped cream cheese, and using a spatula or wooden spoon, fold smoked salmon into the cream cheese until well combined.

5. Serve spread chilled on the Bagel Board (see recipe on page 37) or on its own with bagels, toasted bread, pita chips, or sliced vegetables (cucumbers with this spread are delicious)!

Herb Cream Cheese

SERVES: 8–10

Prep time: 5 minutes | Active time: 5 minutes | Total time: 5 minutes

You can easily enhance the flavor of something as simple as cream cheese with a bundle of fresh herbs. A combination of green scallions, fresh dill, and fresh parsley come together to make this whipped cream cheese more complex, sophisticated, and super spreadable on anything from bagels and crostini to sliced vegetables.

INGREDIENTS

8 ounces cream cheese, softened to room temperature

2 tablespoons green onion, finely chopped

1 tablespoon fresh dill, removed from stem and minced

1 tablespoon fresh parsley, removed from stem and minced

1 tablespoon lemon juice

¼ teaspoon salt

¼ teaspoon pepper

bagels, toasted bread, pita chips, or sliced vegetables, for serving

INSTRUCTIONS

1. Add cream cheese to the bowl of a stand mixer or a mixing bowl.

2. Using a stand mixer or hand mixer with a whisk attachment, mix cream cheese for about 2 minutes until lightly whipped.

3. Add all other ingredients to the whipped cream cheese and whisk with mixer until well combined.

4. Serve spread chilled on the Bagel Board (see recipe on page 37) or on its own with bagels, toasted bread, pita chips, or sliced vegetables.

Fresh Basil Pesto

SERVES: 10–12

Prep time: 5 minutes | Active time: 5 minutes | Total time: 10 minutes

If I succeed in my goal of keeping our basil plant alive all summer long (AJ and I have been able to keep it alive for at least two summers now!) I celebrate our basil abundance with a big batch of fresh pesto. We store a small amount of our homemade pesto to be used for dipping, slathering, or as a sauce in the fridge (homemade pesto keeps for about a week). I freeze the rest in an ice cube tray to give us individual pesto portions into the fall and winter months when our beloved basil plant is long gone (homemade pesto will stay good in the freezer for up to three months).

INGREDIENTS

⅓ cup pine nuts

2–3 cups fresh basil leaves, stems removed

3 cloves garlic, minced

½ cup Parmesan cheese, finely grated

½ cup olive oil

salt and pepper, to taste

crusty bread or fresh vegetables, for serving

You can substitute the basil for your favorite greens or for ones you have on hand: arugula, kale, or oregano will all work in this pesto recipe. Pine nuts can be substituted with walnuts. Store pesto in an airtight jar in the refrigerator for up to one week, or freeze in a small container or ice cube tray for up to three months.

INSTRUCTIONS

1. Toast pine nuts either in the oven or on the stovetop. To toast in the oven, preheat the oven to 375°F. Spread pine nuts out in a single layer on a baking sheet and bake, tossing occasionally, for about 5 minutes until aromatic and golden brown. To toast on the stovetop, spread pine nuts in a dry skillet over medium low heat, stirring frequently, for about 3 minutes until aromatic and golden brown.

2. Place cooled pine nuts and basil leaves into a food processor. Pulse.

3. Add garlic and Parmesan cheese to the food processor. Pulse a few more times and then scrape down the sides with a wooden spoon or rubber spatula so everything is at the bottom.

4. Slowly add olive oil to the food processor. You can add oil in batches and run the food processor in between, or you can slowly pour oil in through the top of the food processor while it's running. You want to slowly add the oil to emulsify the mixture and prevent the oil from separating.

5. Add salt and pepper to taste and pulse to combine.

6. Taste, and add more basil, garlic, Parmesan cheese, or oil to get desired flavor and consistency.

7. Serve as a dip on the Caprese Salad Platter (see recipe on page 22) or to accompany the Caprese Skewers (see recipe on page 121), or spread on crusty bread or fresh vegetables.

Roasted Beet Dip

SERVES: 8–12

Prep time: 5 minutes | Cook time: 1 hour | Active time: 5 minutes | Total time: 1 hour, 10 minutes

When making this vegan, dairy-free dip, keep a few tips in mind when working with beets. The deep purple color of beets stains basically everything it comes into contact with, including countertops, cutting boards, and your fingertips, so work with them on a plastic cutting board while wearing gloves to avoid purple surfaces and fingers. Don't worry about peeling the beets pre-roasting; once the beets are out of the oven and cool enough to touch, put those gloves back on and get to peeling. The skin will easily pull right off.

INGREDIENTS

3 beets

1 head of garlic

¼ cup olive oil

½ teaspoon tarragon

1 teaspoon chives

2 tablespoons orange juice

½ teaspoon orange zest

½ teaspoon salt

vegetables, bread, or crackers, for serving

INSTRUCTIONS

1. Roast the beets and garlic. Preheat oven to 400°F. Wrap each beet individually in aluminum foil and place on a baking sheet.

2. Slice off the top of the head of garlic so individual cloves are exposed, drizzle with a little olive oil, and wrap in aluminum foil. Place garlic on baking sheet.

3. Roast beets and garlic in the oven for about 1 hour until both are soft. Set aside to cool.

4. Once beets are cooled, remove skins and roughly chop. Add beets to a food processor.

5. Squeeze out cloves of garlic into food processor with the beets.

6. Add tarragon, chives, orange juice, orange zest, and salt to food processor. Pulse to combine.

7. Add remaining olive oil to beet mixture and pulse until dip is smooth.

8. Serve with vegetables, bread, or crackers for dipping, or as a part of the Colorful Crudités Platter (see recipe on page 30).

Curried White Bean Dip

SERVES: 8–12

Active time: 5 minutes

Not only do I love the unique, complex flavor that comes from curry powder's combination of spices, and the little kick of heat you get on your taste buds from the cayenne, but I also love that you can pack a punch of flavor with this dip in just five minutes. Using vegetables as your vehicle, this dip is pretty irresistible.

INGREDIENTS

1 (15-ounce) can cannellini beans

2 teaspoons curry powder

½ teaspoon cumin

1 teaspoon dried rosemary

1 teaspoon balsamic vinegar

2 cloves garlic

1 tablespoon lemon juice

¼ teaspoon cayenne pepper

¼ cup olive oil

¼ teaspoon salt or more to taste

vegetables, crackers, pretzels, or bread, for serving

INSTRUCTIONS

1. Drain liquid out of can of beans. Rinse beans with cold water and drain again.

2. Add all ingredients except vegetables, crackers, pretzels, or bread to a food processor. Pulse until well combined and smooth.

3. Serve with vegetables, crackers, pretzels, or bread for dipping. This dip also makes a great addition to the Colorful Crudités Platter (see recipe on page 30)!

Piña Colada Fruit Dip

SERVES: 12–14

Active time: 8–10 minutes | Total time: 8–10 minutes

No matter the season, give your guests a taste of the tropics with this piña colada fruit dip. The flavors of coconut and pineapple always have me daydreaming of soaking up the sun on a warm beach and dipping my toes into crystal clear blue water . . . while sipping on a frozen cocktail, of course! I love this fruit dip for a few reasons: it showcases flavors from one of my favorite tropical cocktails; it's a really quick and easy recipe to make (we're talking just four ingredients and less than ten minutes!); and its creamy sweetness complements a variety of different fruits, everything from apples, bananas, and berries to mango and kiwi.

INGREDIENTS

8 ounces cream cheese, softened to room temperature

1 (7-ounce) jar marshmallow cream

2 tablespoons coconut cream

3 tablespoons pineapple juice

INSTRUCTIONS

1. Add cream cheese and marshmallow cream to the bowl of a stand mixer or a mixing bowl.

2. Using a stand mixer or hand mixer with a whisk attachment, mix cream cheese and marshmallow cream for about 2 minutes until lightly whipped.

3. Shake a can of coconut cream very well and then open using a can opener. Add coconut cream and pineapple juice to the whipped cream cheese mixture and whisk with mixer until well combined.

4. Serve with your favorite pieces of cut fruit or as a part of the Fruit Platter (see recipe on page 33).

Whipped Ricotta

SERVES: 8

Active time: 5 minutes

I was never a big fan of ricotta cheese until I learned of the magic that was created from just five minutes of whipping work. By simply beating ricotta for a few minutes, you transform the (in my opinion) mild, pretty boring, granular cheese into this light, creamy, cloudlike blank canvas for all sorts of flavors. The minimal effort of whipping ricotta is totally worth it to make a super simple but flavorful appetizer that can be served sweet or savory as a standalone dip for fruits, vegetables, bread, or crackers or as a component on a cheese and charcuterie board.

INGREDIENTS

15 ounces whole milk ricotta cheese

3 tablespoons honey

1 tablespoon lemon zest (zest of 1 medium lemon)

fresh fruit or sliced baguette, for serving

INSTRUCTIONS

1. Scoop ricotta into a stand mixer bowl or medium mixing bowl. Using the whisk attachment on a stand mixer or hand mixer, begin to whip the ricotta for 1 to 2 minutes at a medium speed, until it starts to look lighter and fluffy.

2. Slowly add honey and lemon zest to the ricotta while continuously whipping. Whip for a total of about 5 minutes until ricotta is light, smooth and creamy.

3. Serve with fresh fruit or sliced baguette. And don't forget to showcase the sweet version of whipped ricotta on the Red, White & Blue Board (see recipe on page 18), which is full of summer berries just begging to be dipped into some sweet whipped ricotta.

For a savory version of whipped ricotta, omit the honey and add two tablespoons of your favorite herb (such as thyme, rosemary, basil, or parsley) as well as a generous pinch of salt and black pepper.

Bourbon Apple Butter

SERVES: 20–24 (makes 6 half-pint jars)

Prep time: 20 minutes | Cook time: 10 hours | Additional active time: 5 minutes | Total time: 10 hours, 25 minutes

One of my favorite fall activities is going apple picking at a local orchard. Added bonuses of apple picking include enjoying a fall afternoon outside and ending the day with fresh apple cider donuts and hard cider flights. But I always feel like we come home with so many more apples than I know what to do with, and I can only eat so many apples and make so much apple crisp before they start to get bad. Enter the best way to use up a big batch of fresh apples: apple butter! This condiment basically cooks itself (and makes your house smell so good) in the slow cooker, is so delicious slathered on toast or a muffin (it's also great just eating with a spoon) and makes a sweet addition to a seasonal fall cheese and charcuterie board, like the Flavors of Fall Board (see recipe on page 25). It also keeps in the fridge for a couple weeks to a month, if you can even keep it that long without eating it all first.

INGREDIENTS

4 pounds (16 medium or 8 large) apples

½ cup brown sugar

¼ cup maple syrup

1 tablespoon lemon juice

¾ cup bourbon

1 teaspoon cinnamon

1 teaspoon nutmeg

½ teaspoon ground cloves

¼ cup water

½ teaspoon vanilla

INSTRUCTIONS

1. Core and dice apples, leaving skins on.

2. Add apples to a large slow cooker and top with all of the remaining ingredients.

3. Cook on low for 10 hours, stirring occasionally.

4. Once apples are cooked down (the volume of the apples will reduce during the cook time), pureé spiced apples with an immersion blender until smooth. If you don't have an immersion blender, transfer apple mixture to a blender to pureé.

5. Serve as a component on the Flavors of Fall Board (see recipe on page 25) or as a spread for toast or muffins.

I like to prep this recipe before bed and let the apples cook on low in the slow cooker overnight, then blend them in the morning. I divide this recipe into six half-pint mason jars and store in the fridge for 2 to 3 weeks.

Chapter 5

Appetizers & Snacks

As a kid, I remember my parents hosting dinner parties. Our house would fill with people, and laughter would float out of the dining room to the living room where I'd be posted up singing along to my favorite musical or cartoon. Recently, when my mom and I were chatting, I asked her what made the dinner parties stop. "It was a lot of work for me," she said. "I remember always spending a lot of time in the kitchen." This sentiment is exactly why I am a huge fan of small plate or appetizer dining. When AJ and I have people over, we usually ditch the traditional sit-down, multi-course dinner, and instead serve our guests a variety of appetizers, small plates, snacks, and finger foods. A spread of hearty appetizers will not only fill your guests up and give them a diverse menu of flavors and bites to enjoy, but is quicker and easier for you as the host to prepare so you can enjoy the party too. A few tips when it comes to opting for appetizers and snacks rather than a traditional full meal:

- Serve a variety of easy appetizers from different food categories. We like to include something more healthy made with fruits and vegetables like Heirloom Tomato Confit on page 126 or Summer Skewers on page 121, something hearty and starchy like Pepperoni Pinwheels on page 117, something packed with protein like Slow-Cooker Party Meatballs on page 113, Slow-Cooker Buffalo Turkey Meatballs on page 114, or Grilled Shrimp Skewers on page 118, and round everything out with some snacks like Rosemary Garlic Popcorn on page 130, Bacon Fat Party Mix on page 134, Honey-Roasted Almonds on page 146, or Marinated Olives on page 138.

- The more guests you are planning to have, the more appetizer selections you should have. For groups of twelve or fewer, make three to five different appetizers, for groups between thirteen and twenty make five to eight different appetizers, and for groups more than twenty make nine to twelve different appetizers.

- If you aren't going to be serving dinner, you want to make sure your guests leave happy and full, so plan to serve between eight and ten pieces per person.

- Supplement or round out your small plates spread of appetizers and snacks with one of the cheese or snack boards found in Chapter 2 on page 9.

- A day or two before your gathering or party, prep and cook any appetizers or snacks that can be stored in the refrigerator.

Recipe List

Roasted Jalapeño Poppers

SERVES: 8–12 (makes 24 poppers)

Prep time: 10 minutes | Cook time: 25 minutes | Total time: 35 minutes

These jalapeño poppers are the most popular recipe on my blog, so of course I had to include them in my cookbook! Featuring three different cheeses, this recipe is one I've been perfecting for years, and is my go-to game day snack to bring to tailgates and watch parties. I always associate jalapeño poppers with football, just because it's a common appetizer you'll find on the menu at basically every run-of-the-mill sports bar, which makes this spin on the classic appetizer an essential part of the Elevate Your Tailgate Board (see recipe on page 26). Not a sports fan? Not a problem! You don't need a game day to make this popular appetizer. Roasted Jalapeño Poppers are perfect for any party or as a spicy side dish.

INGREDIENTS

12 jalapeño peppers

1 cup (4 ounces) sharp cheddar cheese, shredded

1 cup (4 ounces) feta cheese

4 ounces cream cheese, softened to room temperature

1 teaspoon onion powder

1 teaspoon garlic powder

1 bunch (2 tablespoons) fresh cilantro, coarsely chopped

If you are sensitive to spice and heat, use plastic gloves when cutting and deseeding the peppers to protect your skin. And, if you like things spicy, you can leave the membranes in the jalapeños, as well as a few seeds; those are the source of the heat in the peppers (we think this recipe is plenty spicy with the seeds and membranes removed but you may want to kick it up a notch).

INSTRUCTIONS

1. Preheat the oven to 400°F.

2. Line a baking sheet with parchment paper.

3. Cut the peppers in half and using a small spoon, scrape out the seeds, membranes, and other insides.

4. Add cheeses, spices, and herbs in a bowl and, using the back of a wooden spoon, mash to combine.

5. Using a spoon or clean hands, smear cream cheese mixture into each pepper half. Make sure you do not overstuff the peppers or they will explode in the oven! (If any of the poppers do leak in the oven, spoon the filling back into the pepper while still warm.)

6. Place peppers on baking sheet; put them close to each other to prevent them from rolling around while baking.

7. Bake for 15 to 20 minutes, or until the peppers are tender and the cheese is bubbly.

8. To brown the cheese, broil on high for a few minutes (about 3 to 5 minutes) before removing poppers from the oven. Make sure to keep your eye on the poppers while they are broiling so they don't burn.

9. Serve warm as a part of the Elevate your Tailgate Board (see recipe on page 26) or as a game day or party appetizer!

Pimento Cheese Deviled Eggs

SERVES: 12 (makes 24 deviled eggs)

Prep time: 15 minutes | Cook time: 7–8 minutes | Active time: 20 minutes | Total time: 45 minutes

Deviled eggs are a staple that make an appearance on the menu at almost every party I've ever attended. Christmas? Deviled eggs. Easter? Deviled eggs. Summer potluck? Deviled eggs. Baby or bridal shower? Deviled eggs. And while I do believe deviled eggs have earned our respect and deserve to be a mainstay on basically any party menu (they are always a hit and are usually the first appetizer to get demolished), I prefer to pass on the paprika dusted classic party appetizer and give it a little Southern spin with some creamy, homemade Pimento Cheese (see recipe on page 75).

INGREDIENTS

12 hard-boiled eggs

4 tablespoons mayonnaise

1 teaspoon white wine vinegar

2 teaspoons Dijon mustard

½ teaspoon dry mustard

¼ teaspoon cayenne pepper

¼ teaspoon smoked paprika

¼ teaspoon salt

¼ teaspoon pepper

1½ cups Pimento Cheese (see recipe on page 75)

If you want to prep eggs ahead of time, I recommend hard boiling, peeling, and halving the eggs, as well as scooping out the yolks into a container with a lid the day before you are going to serve them. Store hard-boiled egg halves and yolks separately in the refrigerator and finish the remaining recipe steps on the day you plan to serve them.

INSTRUCTIONS

1. Boil the eggs. Place eggs in a large, deep pot or in two smaller sauce pans (or boil eggs in batches), and cover them with cool water. Cover the pot and bring water to a rolling boil over high heat. When the water starts to boil, reduce the heat to medium high; set a timer for 5 to 6 minutes for a creamy, yellow yolk.

2. Remove pot from heat and let eggs sit in the water for two minutes. Carefully, without dumping out eggs, drain hot water and fill the pot with cold water. Let eggs sit in the cold water for three to five minutes.

3. Once eggs are cool, pat eggs dry, peel off the shell, and halve lengthwise.

4. As you are halving the eggs, use a small spoon to carefully scoop the egg yolks into a mixing bowl. Set boiled egg white halves to the side.

5. Add the mayonnaise, vinegar, Dijon mustard, dry mustard, cayenne pepper, and smoked paprika to the yolks to the mixing bowl. Mash until smooth.

6. Add salt and pepper to taste. Stir to combine.

7. Using a large wooden spoon, spatula, or whisk, mix the pimento cheese into the yolk mixture. Stir until well combined.

8. Scoop the yolk mixture into a pastry bag or quart-size sandwich bag with one corner cut off (a DIY at-home pastry bag) and pipe into the empty egg white halves.

9. Store pimento cheese deviled eggs in the refrigerator until ready to serve. Deviled eggs will keep in the refrigerator for up to one day, but they taste better the day they are made.

Slow-Cooker Party Meatballs

SERVES: 10–12 (makes 20–24 meatballs)

Prep time: 15 minutes | Cook time: 2 hours, 10 minutes | Total time: 2 hours, 35 minutes

These party meatballs, as I like to call them, are in the running for maybe one of the easiest appetizers ever. The sauce has only two ingredients, you can just set and forget them in your slow cooker, and even though the recipe includes ingredients to make the meatballs from scratch, I won't judge you if you make the recipe even easier and use frozen ones. Even though they're simple, they're totally addicting and always a hit at potlucks, holiday parties, game day, or when a sweet and spicy meatball craving hits.

INGREDIENTS

1 pound ground beef

½ white onion, grated

½ cup Panko breadcrumbs

1 egg

½ teaspoon salt

½ teaspoon pepper

1 teaspoon Worcestershire sauce

1 tablespoon olive oil

1 (12-ounce) bottle chili sauce

1 (12-ounce) jar grape jelly

If you don't want to make meatballs from scratch, that's okay! You can use a bag of store-bought frozen meatballs, but increase cooking time to 3 to 4 hours on low to make sure meatballs are fully cooked through.

INSTRUCTIONS

1. Make the meatballs. In a large bowl, combine ground beef, grated onion, breadcrumbs, egg, salt, pepper, and Worcestershire sauce.

2. Using clean hands or a wooden spoon (I prefer to get in there and use my hands!) mix until ingredients are combined, but be careful not to overmix.

3. Roll the ground beef mixture into 1 inch or tablespoon-sized meatballs. Your mixture should yield 20 to 24 meatballs.

4. Brown the meatballs. Add olive oil to a large skillet and heat over medium high heat. Brown the meatballs in batches, cooking about 1 to 2 minutes per side (it usually takes me about 2 to 3 batches to brown all of the meatballs, you don't want to overcrowd the meatballs in the skillet).

5. Transfer browned meatballs to your slow cooker as you finish each batch. The meatballs will not be (and should not be) cooked all the way through after searing them in the pan.

6. While meatballs are browning, add chili sauce and grape jelly to a medium saucepan over medium heat. Whisk to combine and simmer, whisking occasionally, for about 5 minutes until sauce is smooth and grape jelly has no more lumps.

7. Pour the sauce over the meatballs in the slow cooker and gently toss to combine.

8. Cover slow cooker and cook on low for 2 to 3 hours (the meatballs should be cooked through after 2 hours but can stay in the slow cooker on low for up to 3 hours). After 3 hours, change slow cooker setting to warm so meatballs don't overcook.

9. Serve alone as cocktail meatballs with toothpicks or as a component of the Elevate Your Tailgate Board (see recipe on page 26).

Slow-Cooker Buffalo Turkey Meatballs

SERVES: 10–12 (makes 20–24 meatballs)

Prep time: 15 minutes | Cook time: 2 hours, 10 minutes | Total time: 2 hours, 35 minutes

Perfect for game day or even an easy weeknight dinner, buffalo turkey meatballs pack all the flavor of classic buffalo wings and none of the mess! Toss simple turkey meatballs in plenty of hot sauce and let your slow cooker do the work . . . just don't forget lots of blue cheese or ranch for dipping.

INGREDIENTS

1 pound ground turkey

½ cup Panko breadcrumbs

½ white onion, grated

1 egg

2 cloves garlic, minced

½ teaspoon dried oregano

½ teaspoon dried basil

½ teaspoon salt

½ teaspoon pepper

1 tablespoon olive oil

¾ cup buffalo wing sauce

blue cheese and ranch
    dressing, for serving

green onions, diced, for serving

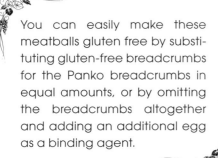

You can easily make these meatballs gluten free by substituting gluten-free breadcrumbs for the Panko breadcrumbs in equal amounts, or by omitting the breadcrumbs altogether and adding an additional egg as a binding agent.

INSTRUCTIONS

1. Make the meatballs. In a large bowl, combine ground turkey, breadcrumbs, grated onion, egg, garlic, oregano, basil, salt, and pepper.

2. Using clean hands or a wooden spoon (I prefer to get in there and use my hands!) mix until ingredients are combined, but be careful not to overmix.

3. Roll the ground turkey mixture into 1 inch or tablespoon-sized meatballs. Your mixture should yield 20 to 24 meatballs.

4. Brown the meatballs. Add olive oil to a large skillet and heat over medium high heat. Brown the meatballs in batches, about 1 to 2 minutes per side (it usually takes me about 2 to 3 batches to brown all of the meatballs. You don't want to overcrowd the meatballs in the skillet).

5. Transfer browned meatballs to your slow cooker as you finish each batch. The meatballs will not be (and should not be) cooked all the way through after searing them in the pan.

6. Add buffalo wing sauce to slow cooker and slowly toss with meatballs to combine.

7. Cover slow cooker and cook on low for 2 to 3 hours. (The meatballs should be cooked through after 2 hours but can stay in the slow cooker on low for up to 3 hours.) After 3 hours, change slow cooker setting to warm so meatballs don't overcook.

8. Serve with blue cheese or ranch dressing drizzled on top or on the side for dipping and a dash of diced green onions if desired. Serve alone as a cocktail meatball or as a less messy wing alternative on the Elevate Your Tailgate Board (see recipe on page 26).

Pepperoni Pinwheels

SERVES: 8–12 (makes 16–24 pinwheels)

Prep time: 10 minutes | Cook time: 20 minutes | Total time: 30 minutes

In college, I would always go to my aunt and uncle's house to cheer on my favorite football team, and every Sunday, my Aunt Julie's Pepperoni Bread was on the menu. The pepperoni bread tradition has continued, long after I graduated and moved away, so much so that Pepperoni Bread is a fall Sunday staple in our house no matter who is playing. Fun fact: pepperoni bread is the most popular appetizer we serve at our annual Super Bowl party . . . it's always the first snack to go.

So of course, I wanted to include a version of the famous and very popular pepperoni bread in this cookbook, so I created these Pepperoni Pinwheels, which are inspired by Aunt Julie's original pepperoni bread recipe, but are handheld to make it easier for guests to grab and serve themselves. Pop a batch in the oven for your next party and serve with plenty of pizza sauce!

INGREDIENTS

1 egg

1 tablespoon water

1 package refrigerated bread or pizza dough

1 teaspoon dried oregano

1 teaspoon dried basil

1 teaspoon garlic powder

¼–½ teaspoon red pepper flakes (depending on how spicy you like things)

8 ounces pepperoni slices

8 ounces mozzarella cheese, shredded

marinara or pizza sauce, for serving

INSTRUCTIONS

1. Preheat oven to 375°F. Spray a muffin tin with cooking spray.

2. Using a whisk or fork, in a bowl whisk egg with water to create an egg wash.

3. On a lightly floured surface, use a rolling pin to roll out bread dough into a large rectangle. Dough should be pretty thin, less than ¼-inch thick.

4. Brush dough with egg wash.

5. Sprinkle oregano, basil, garlic powder, and red pepper flakes evenly across dough.

6. Layer pepperoni slices and mozzarella cheese evenly across bread dough, leaving about ¼ to ½ inch border along all four sides of the dough.

7. Slowly and carefully, tightly roll up the dough lengthwise (hot dog style, if you will). Once rolled into one long log, pinch the ends of the pepperoni roll closed and use a little bit of egg wash to close the seam across the entire roll.

8. With a very sharp knife, slice pinwheels about 1 inch apart.

9. Place individual pinwheels in the muffin tin compartments, one pinwheel per well. Sprinkle with additional spices to taste, if desired.

10. Bake pinwheels for 20 minutes until cheese is melted and pinwheels are golden brown.

11. Serve hot with a side of sauce for dipping.

Grilled Shrimp Skewers

SERVES: 6–8

Prep time: 30 minutes | Cook time: 3–5 minutes | Total time: 33–35 minutes

Every summer, my family spends a week at the beach on the North Carolina coast. It's one of my favorite weeks of the year, but beyond soaking up the sun, watching the waves crash upon the sand, and playing in the surf, I look forward to this annual vacation because of all the seafood we get to eat! These grilled shrimp skewers are inspired by the peel-and-eat shrimp that are a staple at our beach house year after year. They are peeled, cleaned, and marinated ahead of time to save your guests from some of the mess, and then grilled on skewers for simple, utensil-free enjoyment. Serve them hot or cold at any summer soiree . . . ocean breeze not included!

INGREDIENTS

wooden skewers

1 pound shrimp

½ cup olive oil

3 tablespoons Old Bay seasoning

2 tablespoons lemon juice

1 teaspoon garlic powder

INSTRUCTIONS

1. Soak wooden skewers in cold water bath for about 20 minutes to prevent them from burning on the grill.

2. While skewers are soaking, peel and devein shrimp, leaving the tails on if possible. Once all shrimp are peeled and cleaned, thread 4 to 5 shrimp per skewer. Place skewers in a shallow baking dish.

3. In a small bowl, add olive oil, Old Bay, lemon juice, and garlic powder and whisk to combine.

4. Brush each shrimp skewer on each side with Old Bay marinade, and pour remaining marinade on top of the skewers in the baking dish. Place baking dish in the refrigerator and marinate shrimp skewers for at least 30 minutes and up to 1 hour.

5. Preheat grill to medium high heat. Once hot, place shrimp skewers directly on grill and cover and cook for about 90 seconds to 2 minutes. Flip and grill the other side of the shrimp skewers for about 90 seconds to 2 minutes or until shrimp are no longer transparent and pink.

6. Serve warm or cold.

Once cooked, shrimp skewers can be refrigerated covered for up to two days.

Summer Skewers

SERVES: 15–20 (makes 15 skewers of each variety, 45 skewers total)

Prep time: 10 minutes | Active time: 20 minutes | Total time: 30 minutes

When I'm planning a party menu, I like to think about how my guests will be eating. Hosting a sit-down dinner? Then food that needs a fork is totally appropriate. Is this more of a standing room only situation? Then I'm thinking of ways to make sure my guests don't have to awkwardly balance a plate and a cocktail and a set of utensils while also trying to enjoy themselves. Enter my favorite way to eliminate utensils: skewers. Skewers can take any dishes from salads to dessert and easily yet elegantly make them handheld and portable without sacrificing flavor. While I'd probably be willing to put any type of food on a toothpick, the following combinations are my favorite way to showcase summer's bright bounty and bold flavors.

Caprese Skewers

INGREDIENTS

1 pint cherry or grape tomatoes

8–10 ounces mozzarella balls or pearls, patted dry

basil leaves

balsamic glaze, for serving

INSTRUCTIONS

1. Spear the top of a tomato and slide it up near the top of the toothpick or skewer, leaving a bit of room at the top for someone to be able to hold onto the toothpick or skewer. Follow with an individual basil leaf (if your leaves are large, tear them in half) and slide it up the skewer. Repeat with the mozzarella ball. Thread like this for all skewers.

2. Make the balsamic glaze. In a small saucepan over medium heat, simmer ½ cup balsamic vinegar. Once the vinegar begins to bubble, reduce the heat to medium low and simmer until it is reduced by half and thick and syrupy. Remove from heat and set aside.

3. Arrange skewers on a plate or platter for serving. Place the balsamic glaze in a small dish on the platter for dipping.

Watermelon, Feta & Mint Skewers

INGREDIENTS

½ watermelon, halved

mint leaves

8 ounces feta cheese, cubed

balsamic glaze, for serving

INSTRUCTIONS

1. With a melon baller, extract 15 equal sized spheres from the watermelon. If you don't own a melon baller, cut the watermelon into equal sized cubes, about 1 inch big.

2. Spear a watermelon ball or square and slide it up near the top of the toothpick or skewer, making sure to leave some room at the top for someone to hold the skewer. Repeat with a single mint leaf and then a feta cube. Thread like this for all skewers.

3. Make the balsamic glaze. In a small saucepan over medium heat, simmer ½ cup balsamic vinegar. Once the vinegar begins to bubble, reduce the heat to medium low and simmer until it is reduced by half and thick and syrupy. Remove from heat and set aside.

4. Arrange skewers on a plate or platter for serving. Place the balsamic glaze in a small dish on the platter for dipping.

Cantaloupe & Prosciutto Skewers

INGREDIENTS

½ cantaloupe, halved

6–8 ounces prosciutto, sliced

balsamic glaze, for serving

INSTRUCTIONS

1. With a melon baller, extract 15 equal sized spheres from the cantaloupe. If you don't own a melon baller, cut the cantaloupe into equal sized cubes, about 1 inch big.

2. Spear a cantaloupe ball or square and slide it up near the top of the toothpick or skewer, making sure to leave some room at the top for someone to hold the skewer. Repeat with prosciutto. Thread like this for all skewers.

3. Make the balsamic glaze. In a small saucepan over medium heat, simmer ½ cup balsamic vinegar. Once the vinegar begins to bubble, reduce the heat to medium low and simmer until it is reduced by half and thick and syrupy. Remove from heat and set aside.

4. Arrange skewers on a plate or platter for serving. Place the balsamic glaze in a small dish on the platter for dipping.

Devils on Horseback

SERVES: 24 (makes 24 of each variety, 48 total)

Prep time: 30–40 minutes | Cook time: 20–25 minutes | Total time: 50–65 minutes

What's in a name? I've always wondered where one of my favorite party snacks, Devils on Horseback, gets its name. Like, why are these addicting, bacon-wrapped savory bites associated with hell and horses? A little research led me to quite a few theories about the popular appetizer's sinister name, from their diabolical black and red color scheme, to them being a play on the French dish called *anges a cheval* or "angels on horseback" (bacon-wrapped oysters). Even though it seems we can't agree on the etymology of the dish's name, I think we can agree that bacon-wrapped dates stuffed with smoked almonds and goat cheese are irresistibly delicious. And I figured, because I can't say no to a salty, savory bite served on a toothpick, to take a fresh spin on tradition with a no-bake version featuring apricots, goat cheese, walnuts, and prosciutto.

INGREDIENTS

8 slices bacon

6 slices prosciutto

12-ounce package Medjool dates, pitted (yields 24 dates)

1 cup blue cheese crumbles

24 smoked almonds

toothpicks, for serving

7-ounce package dried apricots (yields about 24 apricots)

3 ounces goat cheese

24 walnuts

INSTRUCTIONS

1. Cut bacon and prosciutto slices into thirds, making sure they have enough length to wrap around a date or an apricot.

2. Preheat the oven to 400°F and line a baking sheet with aluminum foil.

3. Halve the dates lengthwise (they should easily pop open along the seam where the pit was removed), being careful not to cut all the way through.

4. Stuff with one almond and, using a spoon or clean hands, a small amount of blue cheese. Wrap a piece of bacon around each date and secure with a toothpick.

5. Place dates on the prepared baking sheet. Bake until bacon is cooked through, 20 to 25 minutes. Transfer dates to a paper towel–lined plate to cool slightly.

6. While the dates are baking, prep the apricot devils on horseback.

7. Place a small walnut and using a spoon or clean hands, a small amount of goat cheese on the center of the apricot.

8. Fold apricot in half, and wrap with a piece of prosciutto. Secure with a toothpick.

9. Serve both hot bacon-wrapped dates and cold prosciutto-wrapped apricots on a platter or plate.

Heirloom Tomato Confit

SERVES: 6–8

Prep time: 10 minutes | Cook time: 1½ hours | Total time: 1 hour, 40 minutes

I love starting my summer Saturdays wandering the stalls at our local farmers' market and stocking up on bright, beautiful, fresh produce. One of my favorite farmers' market creations is this heirloom tomato confit recipe. It screams summer with seasonal tomatoes and fresh herbs from the farmers' market, plus packs a little extra punch of flavor from slowly roasted garlic. The tomatoes, garlic, and herbs need to be roasted low and slow to maximize flavor, so you can just "set it and forget it," making this a super easy, hands-off summer entertaining recipe.

INGREDIENTS

2 pints heirloom cherry tomatoes

2 heads garlic, halved lengthwise

1 cup olive oil

1 bunch (8–10 sprigs) fresh thyme

1 bunch (½–1 cup) fresh basil

crusty bread, for serving

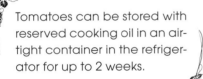

Tomatoes can be stored with reserved cooking oil in an airtight container in the refrigerator for up to 2 weeks.

INSTRUCTIONS

1. Preheat oven to 300°F.

2. Spread tomatoes out in a baking dish in an even, single layer.

3. Place a head of garlic at each end of the dish among tomatoes.

4. Drizzle olive oil on top of tomatoes and garlic.

5. Tuck herbs in different places of the baking dish.

6. Roast the tomatoes low and slow for about 1½ hours or until tomatoes are soft, slightly wrinkled, and blistered.

7. Serve as a component of the Caprese Salad Platter (see recipe on page 22) or simply smear tomatoes on a piece of crusty bread and enjoy.

Spinach & Mushroom Egg Muffins

SERVES: 12

Prep time: 15–20 minutes | Cook time: 30–40 minutes | Total time: 45–60 minutes

Egg muffins are not only tasty, but they're easy to store and reheat, so making a batch of them in advance is a breakfast must whether you're hosting a group of two or a crowd of twenty. And because eggs are basically a blank canvas for all sorts of flavor combinations, you can stick to the spinach and mushroom combo featured here or go crazy and have fun experimenting with a variety of different flavors like broccoli and cheddar, bacon and jalapeño, or even buffalo chicken or sun-dried tomato.

INGREDIENTS

1 tablespoon olive oil

¼ cup onion, finely diced

1 teaspoon salt

1 cup mushrooms, diced

1½ cups spinach, tightly packed

10 eggs

1 tablespoon half-and-half

1 teaspoon garlic powder

½ teaspoon pepper

½ cup Parmesan cheese, shredded

INSTRUCTIONS

1. Heat olive oil in a pan over medium heat. When hot, add onions to the pan, lightly salt them with a pinch of salt, and cook. Stir occasionally until onions are soft and translucent, about 3 to 5 minutes.

2. Once onions are soft, add mushrooms to the same pan and continue to cook onions and mushrooms until the mushrooms are light brown and fragrant, about 3 to 5 more minutes.

3. Add spinach to the pan and cook about 2 minutes until spinach is wilted. Remove from heat and set aside.

4. Preheat the oven to 400°F and lightly spray a twelve-well muffin tin with cooking spray.

5. Crack eggs into a large bowl. Add half-and-half and whisk until eggs are scrambled and half-and-half is combined into the eggs.

6. Season egg mixture with garlic powder, salt, and pepper.

7. Add onion, mushroom, and spinach mixture to the egg mixture and whisk to combine.

8. Add Parmesan cheese to egg mixture. Whisk to combine.

9. Pour egg mixture into muffin tin wells. Divide mixture evenly between all twelve wells, making sure not to overfill. Each well should be filled between ½ and ¾ of the way to the top.

10. Bake egg muffins in oven for 12 to 16 minutes until eggs are set and fully cooked (they will be a yellow to light brown color).

Rosemary Garlic Popcorn

SERVES: 8

Prep time: 5 minutes | Cook time: 5 minutes | Total time: 10 minutes

Popcorn is perfect for parties: it's stupidly simple and crazy quick, even when you pop it the old-fashioned way on the stove. I love taking popcorn beyond the basic run-of-the-mill movie theater melted butter and jazzing it up with a variety of herbs and spices, like this garlic and fresh rosemary blend. Finish it off with a generous sprinkling of freshly grated Parmesan because, in my opinion, cheese makes everything better.

INGREDIENTS

3 tablespoons canola or corn oil

½ cup popcorn kernels

3 tablespoons butter, melted

1½ tablespoons fresh rosemary, removed from stem and finely chopped

1 teaspoon garlic powder

¼ teaspoon salt

¼ cup freshly grated Parmesan cheese

INSTRUCTIONS

1. Pop the popcorn. Heat oil in a heavy bottomed pan over medium high heat. When you think the oil is hot, test the heat of the oil by adding 2 to 3 single popcorn kernels to the oil. When the kernels pop, the oil is hot enough for the popcorn. Add all of the popcorn in a single layer to the pot and cover loosely with a lid, leaving a small space for steam to escape. Gently shake the pot occasionally as popcorn pops (to prevent kernels getting stuck to the bottom and burning). The popcorn is done when you don't hear any more consecutive popping or you are able to count to about 5 seconds in between pops. Pour popped popcorn in a bowl and set aside.

2. In a small microwaveable bowl, melt the butter. Slowly drizzle melted butter over top of the popcorn, tossing gently so the popcorn is evenly coated.

3. Add the rosemary, garlic powder, and salt to the popcorn, tossing gently to combine so the popcorn is evenly coated with the seasonings.

4. Gradually add the Parmesan cheese to the popcorn, tossing gently to combine so the popcorn is evenly coated.

5. Serve as a standalone snack or as a part of the Sweet & Salty Snack Board (see recipe on page 34).

You can use a bag of unflavored popcorn for this recipe; pop the popcorn according to package instructions and pour into a bowl, then add butter and seasonings.

Puppy Chow Popcorn

SERVES: 8

Prep time: 5 minutes | Cook time: 5 minutes | Additional time: 30 minutes | Total time: 40 minutes

Besides watching my mom and grandma in the kitchen, one of my first introductions to cooking was with Ruth, one of my after-school teachers. Mondays were the cooking days at our after-school program; once our homework was done and we'd run on the playground for a while, we'd settle in around a big table with Ruth front and center to lead us in the day's culinary creations. Many of her recipes have stuck with me more than twenty years later, like her unforgettable apple crisp and totally addicting puppy chow. This popcorn is a sweet and salty spin on Ruth's puppy chow (also known in some places as muddy buddies), a kid-friendly snack featuring peanut butter and chocolate and then tossed in a generous helping of powdered sugar.

INGREDIENTS

3 tablespoons canola or corn oil

½ cup popcorn kernels

1 cup semi-sweet chocolate chips

1 cup peanut butter

1 teaspoon coconut oil

2 cups powdered sugar

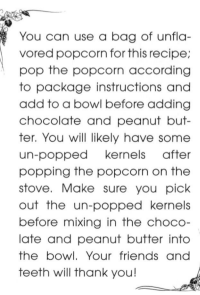

You can use a bag of unflavored popcorn for this recipe; pop the popcorn according to package instructions and add to a bowl before adding chocolate and peanut butter. You will likely have some un-popped kernels after popping the popcorn on the stove. Make sure you pick out the un-popped kernels before mixing in the chocolate and peanut butter into the bowl. Your friends and teeth will thank you!

INSTRUCTIONS

1. Pop the popcorn. Heat oil in a heavy bottomed pan over medium high heat. When you think the oil is hot, test the heat of the oil by adding 2 to 3 single popcorn kernels to the oil. When the kernels pop, the oil is hot enough for the popcorn. Add all of the popcorn to the pot in a single layer and cover loosely with a lid, leaving a small space for steam to escape. Gently shake the pot occasionally as popcorn pops (to prevent kernels getting stuck to the bottom and burning). The popcorn is done when you don't hear any more consecutive popping or you are able to count to about 5 seconds in between pops. Pour popped popcorn in a bowl and set aside.

2. In a microwave safe bowl, add chocolate chips, peanut butter, and coconut oil. Microwave chocolate mixture in 30-second increments; after 30 seconds, remove the bowl from the microwave and stir. Continue to microwave and stir in 30-second increments until chocolate and peanut butter are fully melted (it will take about 2 to 3 times in the microwave).

3. Pour melted chocolate and peanut butter over popped popcorn and stir gently to combine. Dust powdered sugar gradually over chocolate coated popcorn, stirring gently until all of the popcorn is coated in powder sugar.

4. Line a baking sheet with aluminum foil or parchment paper, and pour popcorn onto the baking sheet. Spread it out into an even layer. Chill popcorn on the baking sheet for at least 30 minutes in the fridge until chocolate is set.

5. Serve as a standalone snack or as a part of the Sweet & Salty Snack Board (see recipe on page 34).

Bacon Fat Party Mix

SERVES: 8–10

Prep time: 5 minutes | Cook time: 1 hour, 10 minutes | Total time: 1 hour, 10 minutes

Party snack mix, which was a staple of the slumber parties of my childhood, gets a little update and flavor refresh with this recipe. The secret ingredient is not only crispy bacon, but the fat (or grease) the bacon is cooked in. I love cooking with bacon fat, it adds a nice, salty flavor to everything it touches and gives the run of the mill snack mix I've been chomping on for decades a refreshing and delicious update.

INGREDIENTS

6 slices bacon

3 cups Rice Chex

3 cups Corn Chex

1½ cups mini pretzel twists

1 cup Goldfish or cheddar crackers

¼ cup cashews

¼ cup peanuts

¼ cup walnuts

½ cup bacon grease or butter, melted

3 teaspoons Worcestershire sauce

2 teaspoons garlic powder

1 teaspoon onion powder

1 teaspoon smoked paprika

½–1 teaspoon salt

INSTRUCTIONS

1. Preheat oven to 250°F.

2. Line a large baking sheet with aluminum foil or parchment paper.

3. Cook bacon. In a skillet over medium heat, cook bacon slices until crisp. Once cooled, dice cooked bacon into small pieces. Save the remaining bacon grease.

4. Combine Chex cereals, pretzels, Goldfish, diced bacon, and nuts in a large mixing bowl. Using a large wooden spoon, spatula, or your hands, toss to combine.

5. Melt bacon grease. In a small bowl, add bacon grease and microwave in 30-second increments until completely melted.

6. Add Worcestershire sauce and spices to bacon grease. Stir to combine.

7. Gradually add melted, seasoned bacon grease to the dry ingredients in the large mixing bowl. Stir to coat evenly.

8. Pour cereal mixture onto the lined baking sheet. Spread mixture into an even layer.

9. Bake, stirring every 15 minutes until party mix is toasted and fragrant.

10. Store in an airtight container.

We keep reserved bacon grease in our fridge for cooking, but if you don't, make a big batch of bacon before making this recipe and save the grease (six pieces of bacon will not yield enough bacon grease for this recipe). Butter can be used in the same amount instead of bacon grease, but you will have to add additional salt to the party mix before baking. If you want stronger seasonings, gradually add additional garlic powder, onion powder, and smoked paprika after baking to taste.

Candied Bacon

SERVES: 4–8 (makes 8 large or 16 small slices)

Prep time: 5 minutes | Cook time: 20 minutes | Total time: 25 minutes

Everyone loves bacon, so make the popular breakfast meat a little sweeter with the addition of brown sugar and maple syrup, which creates this amazingly crispy, crackly, caramelized sugar crust.

Serve this sugar coated, salty snack on the Brunch Board (see recipe on page 38), the Flavors of Fall Board (maple and brown sugar really evoke a warm, fall feeling for me, see recipe on page 25) or with some toothpicks for a snack or appetizer. Although I recommend sharing, I won't judge if after you taste it, you want to keep it all for yourself.

INGREDIENTS

8 slices of bacon

⅓ cup brown sugar

3 tablespoons maple syrup

1 teaspoon Sriracha or other hot sauce

INSTRUCTIONS

1. Preheat oven to 375°F.

2. Line baking sheet with aluminum foil and place an oven safe wire rack on top. This will allow bacon to bake evenly.

3. Arrange the bacon in a single layer along the wire rack. Make sure the bacon is evenly spread along the rack and not overlapping or touching (if the bacon is overlapping or touching, use two baking sheets and two wire racks or bake the bacon in two batches).

4. In a small bowl, combine brown sugar, maple syrup, and Sriracha. Mix well.

5. Using a basting brush or spoon, brush brown sugar mixture along each piece of bacon on both sides, dividing the brown sugar mixture evenly among all 8 slices of bacon.

6. Bake bacon in the oven for 18 to 20 minutes until crisp. Check the bacon at about 18 minutes because it can burn quickly if you don't keep your eye on it! The bacon will continue to crisp as it cools.

You can slice the larger bacon strips in half after baking to create smaller bites for your guests.

Marinated Olives

SERVES: 12 (makes 2 cups)

Prep time: 5 minutes | Cook time: 5 minutes | Additional time: 2 hours | Total time: 2 hours, 10 minutes

With just a little effort, and some fresh herbs, spices, and citrus, olives are elevated into the perfect party snack or appetizer that are plump, juicy, and packed full of flavor. These olives are so good that this simple, salty snack has become a fridge staple in our house (AJ will eat them directly from the jar!) and a go-to element of most of my cheese and charcuterie boards.

INGREDIENTS

½ cup olive oil

2½ tablespoons red wine vinegar

2 bay leaves

3 cloves of garlic, smashed and sliced

1 tablespoon fresh rosemary leaves, removed from stem

1 tablespoon fresh thyme leaves, removed from stem

1 teaspoon lemon zest (zest from ½ lemon)

1 teaspoon orange zest

juice from ½ lemon (about 1 tablespoon)

½ teaspoon crushed red pepper flakes (optional)

1 cup green olives, preferably ones that have not been pitted

1 cup Kalamata or black olives, preferably ones that have not been pitted

INSTRUCTIONS

1. In a small saucepan, combine olive oil, vinegar, bay leaves, garlic, rosemary, thyme, and red pepper flakes (if using).

2. Heat over low heat until olive oil mixture is warm.

3. Once warm, remove from heat and stir in lemon and orange zest and lemon juice.

4. Layer both types of olives into a wide-mouth 16-ounce jar with an airtight lid.

5. Slowly pour olive oil mixture over olives until they are covered.

6. Screw the lid on the jar and gently turn jar over a few times to coat olives.

7. Marinate olives. Refrigerate for at least two hours before serving, turning the jar every so often to recoat olives and spread out herbs and seasonings.

8. Take the olives out of the fridge at least one hour prior to serving and transfer the amount you are serving to a small bowl so they can come to room temperature.

9. Serve as a component to a cheese and charcuterie board or as a standalone snack (just make sure you have somewhere for people to put their pits)!

Non-pitted olives work best for this recipe, but you can use pitted olives if you choose. Stay away from olives stuffed with anything (cheese, garlic, pimentos, etc.) to avoid olives getting soggy or flavors that would overpower the herb citrus marinade. Marinated olives can be stored in the refrigerator for up to 2 weeks.

Pickled Jalapeños

SERVES: 16 (makes one 16-ounce jar)

Prep time: 15 minutes | Total time: 15 minutes

My father-in-law has a thriving vegetable garden in his backyard, which always seems to have an abundance of fresh jalapeños. Every summer, the jalapeños seem to grow faster than my in-laws can eat them, and we are always the very lucky recipients of a few mason jars full of spicy pickled jalapeños every time they come to visit. We consistently keep at least one jar of pickled jalapeños in the fridge, and I like to put them on everything: nachos and burgers, in a Bloody Mary, with chicken, in cheese dip (see Chile con Queso recipe on page 60) or Pimento Cheese (see recipe on page 75), or just on their own, straight out of the jar (which is AJ's preferred way of enjoying them).

INGREDIENTS

4 jalapeño peppers, sliced

2 cloves garlic

2½ teaspoons unrefined sea salt

filtered water, enough to fill jar

INSTRUCTIONS

1. Thinly slice jalapeños into rings. If you are sensitive to heat and spice, wear a pair of plastic gloves (or if you don't have plastic gloves, wear two plastic bags over your hands) to protect your hands and fingers during this process. Make sure you wash your hands before touching your eyes!

2. Drop jalapeño slices into a large, 16-ounce jar with an airtight lid. Add garlic and salt to the jalapeños.

3. Pour in enough water to completely submerge the pepper slices. Fill the jar almost to the stop, leaving about 1 inch of space.

4. Cover and seal the jar tightly and turn the jar over several times to mix ingredients.

5. Store the jar at room temperature and away from direct sunlight (a dark, cool place like a pantry or cupboard is perfect) for a week.

6. After 1 week, move the jar to the fridge (they will last a pretty long time in an airtight jar in the fridge, as long as you don't eat them first)!

7. Use pickled jalapeños to spice up dips, as a topping on nachos, burgers, tacos, or enjoy as a spicy snack.

When slicing the jalapeños, remove the seeds and membranes from the jalapeños if you prefer less spice and heat. This is not a canning recipe . . . if you are looking for canning instructions please follow USDA guidelines.

Crispy Spiced Chickpeas

SERVES: 16 (makes 2 cups)

Prep time: 5 minutes | Cook time: 30 minutes | Total time: 25 minutes

Go check your pantry; I bet you have a can of chickpeas in there, especially on that upper shelf or way in the back. Instantly transform your buried-in-the-back-of-the-pantry chickpeas into a salty, savory snack. There are two keys to getting perfectly crisped, spiced chickpeas. First, make sure you rinse and completely dry the chickpeas before putting them in the oven. I keep mine draining on the counter for hours to make sure they are totally dry. Wet chickpeas just don't crisp up as well as dry chickpeas do. And second, wait to add your spice blend until after baking the chickpeas. The taste of your spices can be altered if left too long in the oven, so it's better to toss your chickpeas in the spice blend after roasting, while they're still warm.

INGREDIENTS

1 (15-ounce) can chickpeas

2–3 tablespoons olive oil

½ teaspoon salt

1 teaspoon garlic powder

½ teaspoon cumin

½ teaspoon smoked paprika

½ teaspoon onion powder

⅛–¼ teaspoon cayenne pepper

INSTRUCTIONS

1. Drain and rinse chickpeas. Lay flat on a paper towel or kitchen hand towel to dry. (You want the chickpeas to be completely dry, so I usually let them sit on the towel on the counter for 1 to 1½ hours and give them a fresh paper towel every so often once the one they are draining on is wet.)

2. Preheat your oven to 400°F.

3. Once dried, toss chickpeas in oil and salt.

4. Spread chickpeas in a single, even layer across a baking sheet.

5. Roast chickpeas for 30 minutes until golden brown and firm to the touch.

6. While chickpeas are roasting, combine garlic powder, cumin, smoked paprika, onion powder, and cayenne pepper in a bowl.

7. Once chickpeas are done baking, toss hot chickpeas in spice mixture to coat.

8. Serve as a component on a cheese board or platter, in a salad, or as a party snack all on their own! Chickpeas will taste best the day of cooking, as they tend to lose their crunchy texture as time passes.

If you prefer spicier foods, add ¼ teaspoon cayenne. If you don't prefer spicy foods, add ⅛ teaspoon cayenne or omit entirely.

Cinnamon Sugar Walnuts

SERVES: 16 (makes 2 cups)

Prep time: 5 minutes | Cook time: 20 minutes | Total time: 25 minutes

PSA: Toast your nuts. Just ten minutes in the oven will totally transform any type of nut (walnuts, almonds, pecans, hazelnuts, pine nuts, you get the idea). Toasting nuts gives them a new depth of flavor, preserves their texture (making them stay crisper longer no matter how you use them) and also makes your nuts, and your kitchen, smell amazing. You can take your toasted nuts to the next level (beyond spreading them in a single layer on a baking sheet and sticking them in the over until their browned and toasty) with the addition of simple flavors like sugar, salt, and spice.

INGREDIENTS

1 egg white

1 teaspoon water

1 teaspoon olive oil

2 cups walnuts

2 teaspoons cinnamon

½ cup sugar

pinch of salt

INSTRUCTIONS

1. Preheat oven to 300°F.

2. Add egg white, water, and oil to a mixing bowl. With a whisk or fork, whisk until well combined.

3. Fold walnuts into egg white mixture; stir to combine until walnuts absorb the liquid.

4. In a small bowl, mix together cinnamon, sugar, and salt.

5. Pour cinnamon sugar mixture on top of walnuts and stir to coat the walnuts completely.

6. Spray a baking sheet with cooking spray or coat with oil of your choice. You can also cover your baking sheet with aluminum foil and spray the aluminum foil prior to baking for easy cleanup!

7. Spread walnuts in an even, single layer across baking sheet.

8. Bake 20 minutes or until liquid is set and walnuts are fragrant and crispy.

9. Serve as part of a cheese or charcuterie board such as the Ultimate Cheddar Board (see recipe on page 14), or as a snack on their own!

Honey-Roasted Almonds

SERVES: 16 (makes 2 cups)

Prep time: 5 minutes | Cook time: 15 minutes | Total time: 20 minutes

These Honey-Roasted Almonds will add an extra oomph and completely enhance cheese boards and other platters. They are essential to the UnBrielievable Board on page 17, and would make a great addition to the Sweet & Salty Snack Board on page 34, Red, White & Blue Board on page 18, or Flavors of Fall Board on page 25. You can also serve them as a standalone snack, and they would make a perfect DIY holiday gift or party favor to send home with your guests.

INGREDIENTS

¼ cup brown sugar

½ teaspoon salt

2 cups unsalted almonds (see note box below if using salted almonds)

1 tablespoon olive oil

3 tablespoons honey

½ tablespoon water

¼ teaspoon cinnamon

INSTRUCTIONS

1. Preheat your oven to 350°F.

2. Pour brown sugar and salt into a medium sized bowl, stir to combine, and set aside.

3. Line a baking sheet with parchment paper. Spread almonds in an even, single layer across a baking sheet. Roast in the oven for 10 to 15 minutes until toasted and fragrant.

4. While the almonds are baking, add oil in a small saucepan on medium low heat.

5. Add honey and water to the saucepan and stir to combine.

6. Once honey starts to bubble, add cinnamon and stir to combine.

7. Reduce the heat to low to keep the honey mixture warm.

8. Once almonds are done in the oven, pour baking sheet of almonds into the saucepan with the honey mixture. Over low heat, stir almonds and honey together until the almonds absorb the liquid mixture.

9. Remove almonds from heat and toss into bowl with brown sugar and salt. Toss until well coated.

10. Spread honey-roasted almonds on a baking sheet covered in parchment paper or wax paper to dry and cool. Almonds can be stored covered at room temperature for up to 1 week.

If you are using salted almonds, remove the salt from the brown sugar mixture.

Chapter 6

Cocktails

My first foray into home cocktail making was the summer of 2012 when I was studying for the bar exam. Sure, I had mixed a drink (or two, or more) at home before . . . but do we really count pouring equal parts coconut rum and soda into a solo cup cocktail making? That summer, somewhere between studying and solo cup cocktail making, I decided I deserved a fancy cocktail. So, I muddled some fruit in the bottom of a glass, topped it off with some seltzer and liquor, and a home cocktail connoisseur was born.

Since my at-home cocktail making debut seven years ago, making cocktails at home has become one of my favorite things to do; I love to experiment with what we have in the fridge and our liquor cabinet and play with new drinks and new flavor combinations. AJ and I have made everything from the Classic Margarita (see recipe on page 153) to Spiked Hot Apple Cider (see recipe on page 173). A few at home cocktail making tips:

- Do anything that needs a little work and effort, like making simple syrups or squeezing fresh fruit juice, ahead of time. Like one to two days ahead of time. You can store ingredients in a mason jar or other container in the fridge and use as necessary.

- When mixing cocktails for a crowd, scale the recipe and then make a big batch cocktail in a pitcher or a punch bowl (again, preferably ahead of time). All the recipes in this book can easily be doubled or tripled (or even more) to serve a crowd. Making cocktails in a big batch will save you time and energy and keep you from having to mix up individual cocktails all night.

- Don't be afraid to let your guests do some of the work. I'll often batch my mixer without alcohol (like in the Spicy Bloody Mary recipe on page 170 or the Sparkling Raspberry Lemonade Punch recipe on page 157) and then have my guests add in their preferred amount of spirits or wine or prosecco as they pour their own cocktail. This method also then caters to your friends or family who don't drink, giving them a drink option beyond the standard soda or water options.

Recipe List

These cocktails can easily be batched for a larger crowd by squeezing fresh lime juice in a large batch ahead of time (or using store-bought lime juice) and storing it in the refrigerator.

Classic Margarita

SERVES: 2

Prep time: 5 minutes | Total time: 5 minutes

I will forever and ever associate margaritas with my best friend, Tina, because it was what I ordered when she and my mom took me out for a drink on my 21st birthday and it was the cocktail we made on repeat when we lived together in graduate school. Lots of margarita mix and blending was involved. (Oh, and lots and lots of tequila.) When it comes to margaritas now, long gone are the days of blenders and margarita mix, but I do always think of Tina when I whip up one of these easy, freshly squeezed beauties. These simple margaritas are one of our favorite cocktails to make at home no matter the reason, and with just four ingredients and five minutes, they've made store-bought mix obsolete.

INGREDIENTS

lime wedge, for the glass rim and for garnish

salt, for the glass rim

4 ounces tequila

2 ounces triple sec or orange liquor (see note box below)

3–4 ounces fresh squeezed lime juice (approximately 3–4 limes)

fresh squeezed orange juice to taste (approximately ½ orange)

INSTRUCTIONS

1. When selecting fresh limes to use in this recipe, pick firmer limes rather than soft limes (soft limes have less liquid in them). Rub a lime on the outer edge of two cocktail glasses and dip the rim of the glasses into salt. Set aside.

2. Combine tequila, orange liquor, lime, and orange juice in a cocktail shaker with ice. Shake until chilled and well blended.

3. Put fresh ice into the salt-rimmed glasses, strain, and pour cocktails from the shaker into the glasses.

4. Garnish with lime wedge or wheel.

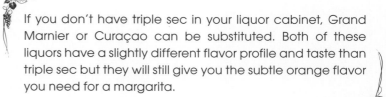

If you don't have triple sec in your liquor cabinet, Grand Marnier or Curaçao can be substituted. Both of these liquors have a slightly different flavor profile and taste than triple sec but they will still give you the subtle orange flavor you need for a margarita.

Watermelon Frosé

SERVES: 5–7

Prep time: 10 minutes | Cook time: 5 minutes | Additional time: 2 hours | Total time: 2 hours, 15 minutes

It gets so sweltering hot in North Carolina in the summer (like surface of the sun hot) the only way to survive is with a steady stream of air conditioning and a cooling cocktail. Enter one of my favorite summertime treats: Watermelon Frosé. Frosé is exactly what it sounds like: simply put, frozen rosé wine. It's super popular in bars and restaurants but you can also easily make it at home, sans slushee machine. To add some natural sweetness, I like to blend chilled rosé wine with one of my favorite summer fruits, frozen watermelon, and a splash of lime to create a refreshing cocktail you'll want to sip on all summer long.

INGREDIENTS

4 cups frozen watermelon

1 bottle rosé wine

juice of 4 limes

2 tablespoons sugar (optional)

INSTRUCTIONS

1. Cube watermelon and freeze about four cups of watermelon cubes.

2. Once frozen, put about ½ the wine and ½ the watermelon cubes into blender. Blend until smooth. (You can make a nonalcoholic version by simply omitting the wine and adding sparkling water.)

3. Evaluate consistency and add more frozen watermelon or wine and blend again.

4. Continue slowly adding until you get desired consistency. Blend in lime juice and sugar, if using.

Add the sugar or some simple syrup if you like sweeter cocktails.

Sparkling Raspberry Lemonade Punch

SERVES: 12–14

Prep time: 5 minutes | Total time: 5 minutes

This Sparkling Raspberry Lemonade Punch has been a huge hit at many a bridal and baby shower. What I love about this punch, besides the fact that in comes together in less than five minutes with just three ingredients, is that first, it always gives me an excuse to use our crystal punch bowl and matching glasses, a set inspired by my grandmother's glassware given to us as a wedding gift from my mom. And second, it's a nonalcoholic punch, which is perfect for kids, nondrinkers, and mamas-to-be (again, a perfect baby shower beverage)! But with little effort and a quick splash of champagne or vodka, you easily have a cocktail version.

INGREDIENTS

4 (12-ounce) cans or bottles ginger beer, chilled

4 cups (32 ounces) lemonade, chilled

2 cups (16 ounces) frozen raspberries

ice, as needed

INSTRUCTIONS

1. In a large punch bowl or pitcher, mix the ginger beer and lemonade.

2. Just before serving, remove raspberries from freezer and add to punch. As the punch sits out, you may need to add ice as needed, but the frozen raspberries will keep the punch cool to start.

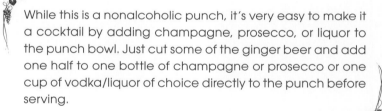

While this is a nonalcoholic punch, it's very easy to make it a cocktail by adding champagne, prosecco, or liquor to the punch bowl. Just cut some of the ginger beer and add one half to one bottle of champagne or prosecco or one cup of vodka/liquor of choice directly to the punch before serving.

Blackberry-Basil Gin Fizz

SERVES: 2

Prep time: 5 minutes | Active time: 5 minutes | Total time: 10 minutes

My dad is more of a cold beer guy than a cocktail guy, but when he does have a cocktail, it's always in the summertime and it's always a gin and tonic. Extra ice, extra lime. My dad's simple summertime sippers inspired this Blackberry-Basil Gin Fizz. The addition of seasonal blackberries and basil not only complement but also cut gin's bold flavors (if you're in the "gin tastes like a Christmas tree" camp, you need to try this drink before writing off gin forever). Muddle the two with some honey, fill a glass with ice, and don't forget a few extra squeezes of lime!

INGREDIENTS

1 cup blackberries (about 14–16 blackberries)

6–8 basil leaves, removed from stems, plus more for garnish

juice of 2 limes

2 tablespoons honey

4 ounces gin

ice, as needed

seltzer water or club soda, as needed

INSTRUCTIONS

1. Place blackberries, basil, lime juice, and honey into a cocktail shaker and muddle together by pressing down on the fruit and herbs lightly with a cocktail muddler or spoon and giving a few gentle twists. You should see juice squirting out from the blackberries.

2. Pour gin into the cocktail shaker.

3. Add ice to the shaker and shake until chilled and well combined.

4. Fill two cocktail glasses with crushed ice.

5. Strain blackberry-basil mixture into the two glasses, or if you're like us and prefer to enjoy the bits of blackberries and basil that are a result of the muddling, don't use a strainer when transferring to the cocktail glasses.

6. Top each cocktail with seltzer water or club soda.

7. Garnish with fresh basil leaves.

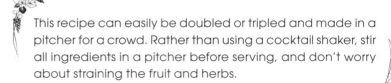

This recipe can easily be doubled or tripled and made in a pitcher for a crowd. Rather than using a cocktail shaker, stir all ingredients in a pitcher before serving, and don't worry about straining the fruit and herbs.

Beer Cocktail Float

SERVES: 8–10

Prep time: 20 minutes | Cook time: 5 minutes | Additional time: 2 hours | Total time: 2 hours, 25 minutes

As a kid, ice cream floats were one of my favorite summertime treats. Cold vanilla ice cream bobbing around in a glass of frothy root beer was a sweet and creamy concoction I craved, especially after a long day at the pool or beach. As an adult, I still can't say no to a really refreshing root beer float, but I also thought it'd be fun to put a more mature spin on one of my favorite childhood treats by adding a little cold beer to the mix.

INGREDIENTS FOR THE GRANITA

¾ cups sugar

3 cups water

1–1½ cups freshly squeezed lime juice (the juice of about 8 limes)

1 teaspoon grated lime zest

INGREDIENTS FOR THE BEER FLOAT

2–3 scoops homemade lime granita (see instructions for the granita below)

1 (12-ounce) bottle of your favorite light beer, per cocktail

splash of pineapple juice, per cocktail

INSTRUCTIONS FOR THE GRANITA

1. Pour sugar and water into a small saucepan over medium heat. Stir to combine and bring to a boil. Reduce heat and simmer for about 5 minutes.

2. Remove saucepan from heat and allow to cool to room temperature for about 1 hour.

3. Stir in lime juice and zest.

4. Pour the granita mixture into a shallow metal pan and freeze for 2 to 3 hours. Every 30 minutes, remove the pan from the freezer and scrape and stir any large chunks with the tines of a fork. This will give the granita a slushy texture that is not solid ice and you should be able to scoop with a spoon.

INSTRUCTIONS FOR THE BEER FLOAT

1. Scoop 3–4 spoonsful of granita into a cocktail or pint glass.

2. Pour chilled beer over lime granita and top with a splash of pineapple juice.

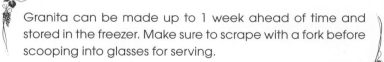

Granita can be made up to 1 week ahead of time and stored in the freezer. Make sure to scrape with a fork before scooping into glasses for serving.

Prosecco Pop Cocktail

SERVES: 6

Prep time: 15 minutes | Cook time: 20 minutes | Additional time: 24 hours, 20 minutes | Total Time: 24 hours, 55 minutes

A few summers ago, I discovered these super cute, super refreshing prosecco popsicle cocktails at a trendy rooftop bar in Charlotte, going for $14 a pop (both literally and figuratively). Because I am not one to turn down a creative summer cocktail that consists of a fruit popsicle melting into my glass of bubbles, I of course paid the $14 for my drink, then promptly made a promise to myself that I'd figure out how to replicate it at home.

INGREDIENTS FOR THE POPSICLES

16 ounces strawberries, hulled

2 cups water, divided

1 cup sugar

1 cup lemon juice

INGREDIENTS FOR THE COCKTAILS

6 strawberry lemonade popsicles

1 bottle prosecco or champagne, chilled

I like making homemade popsicles (and have invested in a $10 popsicle mold that we use all summer long) but you can totally use store-bought popsicles for this recipe. I would recommend seeking out and paying for more high-quality store-bought popsicles made with fresh fruit as they will make your cocktails taste better.

INSTRUCTIONS FOR THE POPSICLES

1. Add strawberries, 1 cup of water, and sugar to a saucepan. Bring to a boil over medium high heat.

2. Once boiling, reduce heat to low and cover the saucepan. Simmer strawberries for 10 minutes.

3. Using an immersion blender, blend strawberry-sugar mixture until smooth. If you don't have an immersion blender, allow mixture to cool and then transfer to a blender to blend.

4. Allow mixture to cool for about 20 to 30 minutes.

5. In a pitcher or mason jar, mix lemon juice, remaining water, and strawberry syrup. Add additional lemon juice or water to taste.

6. Pour strawberry lemonade into popsicle molds. Do not overfill molds, leaving about ¼ inch of space at the top of each mold for expansion. Freeze overnight.

INSTRUCTIONS FOR THE COCKTAILS

1. Fill half of a wine glass with prosecco and place a popsicle in the glass.

2. Let the popsicle melt a little before serving.

This recipe picture features three different fruit purées: strawberry, blackberry, and peach. Make a variety of fruit purées and set up a Bellini Bar to allow your guests to pick their favorite flavors. And don't shy away from mixing flavors together . . . doesn't a blackberry peach bellini sound delicious?

Fruit Bellini

SERVES: 5–6

Prep time: 10 minutes | Cook time: 25 minutes | Total time: 35 minutes

Pop some prosecco for fruit bellinis! These sweet, seasonal sippers are the perfect party beverage for spring and summertime celebrations like at-home brunch, baby showers, and bridal showers. Bookmark this page if you're hosting Easter brunch or a special springtime celebration soon! Bellinis can be made with a few different ingredients like berries and peaches, so offer a variety of fruit purées and set up a Bellini Bar to allow your guests to mix and match flavors and create their own perfect champagne cocktail. Make sure to have a little plain sparkling water or club soda on hand to create a mocktail version as well!

INGREDIENTS

2–3 cups strawberries, blackberries, blueberries, raspberries, or peaches

2 teaspoons sugar

1 teaspoon lemon juice (juice of ½ lemon)

1 teaspoon water

1 bottle champagne, prosecco, or bubbly wine, chilled

INSTRUCTIONS

1. Make the fruit syrup. If using strawberries or peaches, slice strawberries in half and dice peaches. If using other berries, you can leave them whole. Place fruit in a small sauce pan with sugar, lemon juice, and water.

2. Heat saucepan on medium heat. Once fruit mixture is boiling, reduce heat to low and simmer for 25 minutes, stirring occasionally to prevent fruit from sticking to the saucepan. Remove from heat when fruit has a syrupy consistency. Cool.

3. Once cooled, purée fruit with an immersion blender or transfer to a blender to purée.

4. Make the bellinis. Pour a small amount (about 1 to 2 tablespoons) of fruit purée in the bottom of a champagne flute or wine glass. Top with champagne, prosecco, or wine. Amounts can be adjusted to taste.

If you prefer sweeter cocktails, add 1 tablespoon of sugar rather than 2 teaspoons.

Red Wine Sangria

SERVES: 6–8 (makes 1 pitcher)

Prep time: 10 minutes | Active time: 5 minutes | Total time: 15 minutes

The summer after I graduated college, I spent a week in Barcelona with one of my best friends, wandering the streets and staring at all the Gaudi we could. Besides the history, culture, and art, I loved Barcelona because of, of course, the food. And the fact that you could always get a carafe of red sangria from a sidewalk café anywhere in the city. This Red Sangria recipe is a nod to the summer evenings I spent sipping sangria and stuffing myself with paella in Barcelona's picturesque plazas; it's made with Spanish red wine (of course!), lots of citrus, and a cinnamon stick, which was always floating in our sangria carafes.

INGREDIENTS

1 lemon, sliced

1 lime, sliced

1 orange, sliced

2 tablespoons honey

1 apple, diced

¾ cup pomegranate seeds

⅓ cup triple sec

½ cup orange juice

1 bottle red wine, chilled

1 cinnamon stick

INSTRUCTIONS

1. Add lemon, lime, and orange slices to the bottom of a pitcher. Pour honey on top and gently muddle with a muddler or wooden spoon until citrus juices release and honey is incorporated.

2. Add apple and pomegranate seeds. Stir to combine.

3. Add triple sec and orange juice. Stir to combine.

4. Pour in bottle of red wine. Stir to combine.

5. Add cinnamon stick. Stir to combine.

6. Refrigerate until ready to serve. Wait at least 1 to 2 hours before serving for cinnamon stick to infuse sangria. Sangria will keep in the fridge for up to 2 days.

I prefer to use a low tannin red wine like Grenache or Pinot Noir in red sangria because they taste the best chilled.

White Wine Sangria

SERVES: 6–8 (makes 1 pitcher)

Prep time: 5-10 minutes | Active time: 5 minutes | Total time: 10-15 minutes

Batch cocktails are key for a crowd. Sangria is a classic example of a batch cocktail: add all of the ingredients to a pitcher and the flavor will develop over time. Keep a few bottles of white wine and some extra fruit chilled in the fridge to replenish the pitcher as necessary, but otherwise this summer refresher is pretty much hands off.

INGREDIENTS

1 lemon, sliced

1 lime sliced

1–2 ripe peaches, sliced

1 cup raspberries

1 cup blackberries

¼ –½ cup peach schnapps (½ cup will make your sangria a little bit stronger and sweeter)

1 bottle dry, crisp white wine (Sauvignon Blanc or Pinot Grigio are my top choices), chilled

honey or sugar, as needed

ice, as needed

sparkling water or club soda, as needed

INSTRUCTIONS

1. Add lemon, lime, peaches, raspberries, and blackberries to a large pitcher. Muddle fruit at the bottom of the pitcher with a muddler or large wooden spoon so they are soft and release some of their juices.

2. Add peach schnapps and muddle again.

3. Add chilled white wine and stir to combine.

4. Taste and adjust based on your personal preferences. For more sweetness, add a little peach schnapps, some honey, or sugar. For more acidity, add a squeeze of lemon or lime juice.

5. Serve cold over ice. Sangria can be stored covered in the fridge for up to 48 hours.

If you prefer your cocktails a little sweeter, add 1–2 teaspoons of sugar or honey to the pitcher when you add the fruit and muddle together. To dilute the cocktail, serve in a glass topped with sparkling water or club soda.

Spicy Bloody Mary

SERVES: 6

Active time: 5 minutes | Additional time: 24 hours | Total time: 24 hours, 5 minutes

With a reputation as a restorative or "hair of the dog" drink, a Bloody Mary is the quintessential morning cocktail. It is a staple in our house on Black Friday and New Year's Day, but you can also make a batch of this popular brunch beverage for morning gatherings like a baby or bridal shower, holidays, or tailgates. Let guests customize their drinks with a variety of spices and garnishes using the Build-Your-Own Bloody Mary Board (see recipe on page 41).

INGREDIENTS

4 cups tomato juice

3 tablespoons pickle juice

1 teaspoon hot sauce

3 teaspoons Worcestershire sauce

1 tablespoon lemon juice

½ teaspoon dried oregano

½ teaspoon dried basil

½ teaspoon garlic powder

2 teaspoons creamy prepared horseradish

1 teaspoon celery salt

1 teaspoon Old Bay seasoning, plus 1 tablespoon for the salt rim

¼ teaspoon salt, plus ¼ teaspoon for the rim

¼ teaspoon pepper

lime or lemon wedge, for the rim

2 ounces vodka or gin, per cocktail

INSTRUCTIONS

1. Add all ingredients except ingredients for the rim and liquor to a large pitcher, carafe, or mason jar. Stir to combine.

2. Taste and adjust seasonings to your preference (you may want to add additional hot sauce, Old Bay, lemon juice, garlic, salt, or pepper).

3. Chill mix in the refrigerator overnight (this allows the flavors to better come together and the mix will taste better)!

4. Make the salt rim. On a shallow plate, combine Old Bay and salt. Prior to filling a glass with ice, make a notch in a quarter of a lime or lemon. Rub the notch along the top rim of the glass until rim is wet. Tip the glass into the Old Bay and salt mixture and spin until the rim is coated.

5. Make the cocktail. In a glass with plenty of ice, combine 5 ounces Bloody Mary mix and 2 ounces vodka or gin. Stir to combine. Garnish as desired.

Bloody Mary mix will keep in the fridge for up to 1 week.

Spiked Hot Apple Cider

SERVES: 5–6

Prep time: 2 minutes | Cook time: 10 minutes | Total time: 12 minutes

Spiked hot apple cider screams fall in its flavors, making it the perfect cocktail to celebrate changing leaves and chilly nights. This cozy cocktail is as simple as simmering some cider with warming spices, and then adding a little extra kick with vanilla- or cinnamon-infused bourbon (you can either buy the bourbon already flavored at the store or infuse it yourself). We love to sip on this warm cider all fall long whether it be on camping trips, during an evening around the fire pit in our backyard, or as a nightcap after our family's Thanksgiving feast.

INGREDIENTS FOR THE INFUSED BOURBON

3–4 vanilla bean pods or
   3–4 cinnamon sticks

3 cups (750 ml) bourbon

INGREDIENTS FOR THE COCKTAIL

5 cups apple cider

1 stick cinnamon

3 whole cloves

2 star anises

2 ounces vanilla- or cinnamon-
   bourbon, per cocktail

cinnamon sticks for garnish

INSTRUCTIONS FOR THE INFUSED BOURBON

1. If using vanilla bean pods, split the pods lengthwise. Divide bourbon among two large 16-ounce airtight jars. Submerge vanilla bean pods or cinnamon sticks into the bourbon. Store in a cool, dry place for 1 to 2 weeks, shaking the jars occasionally to mix the spices. Taste after one week to determine the flavor intensity. The bourbon is done infusing when it tastes good to you.

INSTRUCTIONS FOR THE COCKTAIL

1. Make the apple cider. Pour the apple cider into a small saucepan or pot. Add cinnamon, cloves, and star anise to the pot and bring to a boil.

2. Once boiling, reduce heat to medium low or low and simmer for 5 to 10 minutes.

3. Remove cider from heat and strain into a thermos or a pitcher.

4. Make the cocktail. Pour 1 cup cider mix and 2 ounces infused bourbon into a cocktail glass.

5. Garnish with a cinnamon stick.

You do not need to make your own flavored bourbon. Feel free to purchase flavored bourbon, if available, at your local liquor or grocery store.

Pumpkin Old Fashioned

SERVES: 1

Prep time: 5 minutes | Active time: 10 minutes | Total time: 15 minutes

No one says pumpkin drinks have to be served hot, so why not enjoy the flavors of fall over ice when the calendar says its fall but the weather strikingly resembles summer? This Pumpkin Old Fashioned packs a lot of pumpkin punch with just a splash of pumpkin simple syrup without bringing any extra heat (it's served over a large ice cube, after all), giving you a refreshing taste of fall no matter what Mother Nature says.

INGREDIENTS FOR THE PUMPKIN SIMPLE SYRUP

1 cup water

1 cup brown sugar

1 vanilla pod or 1 teaspoon vanilla extract

½ can (8 ounces) pure pumpkin

½ teaspoon ground cinnamon

¼ teaspoon ground ginger

¼ teaspoon ground nutmeg

¼ teaspoon ground cardamom

INGREDIENTS FOR THE OLD FASHIONED

ice, as needed

2 ounces of your favorite bourbon or whiskey

¼ ounce pumpkin simple syrup (see recipe)

1–2 dashes angostura or orange bitters

INSTRUCTIONS FOR THE PUMPKIN SIMPLE SYRUP

1. In a small saucepan over medium heat, add the water and brown sugar and stir to combine. Stir occasionally as sugar-water heats up to dissolve the sugar into the water.

2. Once sugar is dissolved, bring the sugar-water mixture to a brief boil and reduce the heat to medium low and simmer for 2 minutes.

3. If using vanilla pod, using a sharp knife, slice the vanilla pod open and scrape out the vanilla beans. Add pumpkin, cinnamon, ginger, nutmeg, cardamom, and vanilla beans or vanilla extract (if using) to sugar-water mixture. Simmer another 2 to 3 minutes, stirring occasionally, and then remove from heat.

4. Cover the saucepan to allow simple syrup to steep while cooling.

5. Once cooled, using a mesh strainer or cheesecloth, strain simple syrup into an airtight jar, and store in the refrigerator up to 1 week.

INSTRUCTIONS FOR THE OLD FASHIONED

1. In a rocks glass with 1 large ice cube or your preferred amount of cubed ice, add 2 ounces of your favorite bourbon, ¼ ounce pumpkin simple syrup, and a few dashes of bitters.

A classic old fashioned traditionally features a sugar cube or granulated sugar. Because the pumpkin simple syrup features a 1:1 sugar to water ratio, the ¼ ounce of pumpkin simple syrup in this recipe is equivalent to the 1 sugar cube or 1 teaspoon of sugar that an old fashioned usually calls for. If you prefer sweeter cocktails you can add additional pumpkin simple syrup up to 1 ounce.

Cranberry Sauce Mule

SERVES: 1

Active time: 5 minutes

Even though I love making (and eating) cranberry sauce, maybe my family doesn't love cranberry sauce as much as I do, because we always seem to have an abundance of cranberry sauce left after Thanksgiving dinner. Last year, as the cranberry sauce sat sadly in our fridge, I had an idea of how to repurpose it: cocktails! The sugary sauce is the perfect mixer in a mule because it acts as a flavored simple syrup. Add a few ounces of vodka; a few squeezes of lime, and ginger beer and you've got yourself a festive cocktail and a way to use up your cranberry sauce.

INGREDIENTS

2 tablespoons leftover sweetened homemade or store-bought cranberry sauce

2 ounces vodka

½ lime

ice, as needed

4–6 ounces ginger beer (depending on how strong you like your cocktails)

whole cranberries, for garnish

fresh rosemary sprigs, for garnish

INSTRUCTIONS

1. Add cranberry sauce, vodka, and lime juice to the bottom of a cocktail shaker.

2. Add ice to the cocktail shaker and shake until well combined and the shaker is cold.

3. Fill a copper mug or cocktail glass with crushed or whole ice cubes. Pour contents of the cocktail shaker into the mug or glass.

4. Top cranberry vodka mixture with 6 ounces of ginger beer. Stir to combine.

5. Garnish with fresh whole cranberries and a rosemary sprig.

Sweetened cranberry sauce acts as a sweet, simple syrup in this cocktail. If you don't have cranberry sauce on hand, you can substitute 2 ounces of unsweetened cranberry juice and 1 ounce of simple syrup or honey.

Acknowledgments

To Nicole Mele and the Skyhorse Team: Thank you for believing in me and trusting me to bring this project to life. I have appreciated all of your guidance, expertise, encouragement, and feedback throughout this process, and although it has been a lot of work, it has been rewarding and fulfilling. I have grown as a recipe developer and writer because of you.

To Mom and Dad: Thank you for instilling a love of reading and writing. Thank you for teaching me the value of really hard work; this book (and the rest of my life's accomplishments) is a direct result of your inspiration and motivation. Thank you for always being supportive and enthusiastic of my crazy ideas, for being my number one fans, for leading by example, and for always being there for me. Thank you for sharing your invaluable feedback, experience, and expertise as I went through this process; you're the people I always go to first when I need advice, feedback, or editing. I love you both so much.

To Katie: Thank you for being the best sister a girl could ever ask for. Thank you for motivating me when I was hesitant to take this on and telling me I could do it. Thank you for cheering me on, for being there when I need to talk or bounce ideas off of you, for making me laugh, for letting me take pictures of your food before you eat it, for everything you do for me, big or small. Your creativity, compassion, and hard work inspires me and pushes me to be better not only professionally but as a sister and friend. And thank you for being the best baker in the family and making delicious pie.

To AJ: Thank you for encouraging me to tackle this project even though we had a zillion other things going on in our lives, and your seemingly endless amount of patience while I was working on it. Thank you for hand modeling, taste testing, dishwashing, photo reviewing, eating your food when it's cold, making me laugh, loving me, and so much more. I know you'll always help and support me, even if it comes with a side of eye roll. I love experiencing, navigating, and living life with you.

To Tina and John: Thank you for your enthusiasm, love, and letting me use you as taste testers.

To my friends: Thank you for all of your encouragement, support, and enthusiasm about this book. I am so lucky to be surrounded by a community of smart, strong women both near and far. You all are a constant inspiration to me.

To the Mecklenburg County Public Defender's Office: Thank you for giving me a job; without it, I would have never moved to Charlotte, which sparked my idea for my blog, which gave me the opportunity to write this cookbook. But more importantly, thank you for giving me the opportunity to do really good work that I love, for being strong and passionate defenders of justice, and for fighting for fairness and equality. I love being a part of such a smart, talented, and caring group of people, many of whom have become lifelong friends.

To my blogging friends: Thank you to all of the friends I've met on the Internet for welcoming me with open arms, and for your camaraderie, motivation, inspiration, and support, especially to Mary for inviting me to that first lunch and introducing me to the Charlotte food blogging community; LeAndra for our dinner dates and being an outlet to bounce around ideas; and Tiffany for generously dedicating your time to answer all of my questions and sharing your experience and expertise. I am grateful to be a part of such a fun, creative, and supportive community.

To my readers: Thank you for reading my blog, recreating my recipes at home, asking for restaurant recommendations and travel tips, taking a class, liking, commenting, emailing, and supporting *Off the Eaten Path* in many different ways. Seven years ago, when I was bored and lonely and started writing about what I was eating, I never imagined this is where *Off the Eaten Path* would take me; I wouldn't and couldn't be here without you.

To Central Coffee: Thank you for letting me post up for hours while I endlessly typed away on my laptop and for making the best chai latte in all of Charlotte, North Carolina.

To Lizzo: Thank you for providing me with an endless, uplifting soundtrack for photo shoots.

To Pheebs and Bodie: Thank you for being by my side during every single photo I took for this book. I would say you're the best photo assistants, but you mostly get in the way and sleep on the job. I love you.

About the Author

Chrissie Nelson Rotko is the writer and photographer behind the popular food and travel blog, *Off the Eaten Path*, which she initially created in 2013 to combine her love of food and writing. Her work on *Off the Eaten Path* has been recognized both locally and nationally by a variety of outlets and publications, including *Zagat* and *Charlotte* magazine. Chrissie also teaches classes about blogging and social media, and has appeared regularly on local television.

In addition to running her food business, Chrissie works full-time as an assistant public defender, where she enjoys working one-on-one with clients, representing them in court, and being a part of the passionate and dedicated community that her colleagues have created. She graduated from Lawrence University and the University of Wisconsin Law School before moving to Charlotte, North Carolina, where she lives with her husband, AJ, rescue dog, Bodie, and four cats: Phoebe, Mr. Kitty, Brett Favre, and Princess.

When she's not writing or taking photos of her kitchen creations, Chrissie loves visiting local restaurants and craft breweries, traveling, taking weekend road trips with AJ and Bodie, hanging out with her family and friends, and spending time outdoors, especially at the beach.

You can read Chrissie's blog at www.offtheeatenpathblog.com and follow along with her culinary and travel adventures on Instagram @chrissie_beth.

Conversion Charts

METRIC AND IMPERIAL CONVERSIONS

(These conversions are rounded for convenience)

Ingredient	Cups/Tablespoons/Teaspoons	Ounces	Grams/Milliliters
Butter	1 cup/ 16 tablespoons/ 2 sticks	8 ounces	230 grams
Cheese, shredded	1 cup	4 ounces	110 grams
Cream cheese	1 tablespoon	0.5 ounce	14.5 grams
Cornstarch	1 tablespoon	0.3 ounce	8 grams
Flour, all-purpose	1 cup/1 tablespoon	4.5 ounces/0.3 ounce	125 grams/8 grams
Flour, whole wheat	1 cup	4 ounces	120 grams
Fruit, dried	1 cup	4 ounces	120 grams
Fruits or veggies, chopped	1 cup	5 to 7 ounces	145 to 200 grams
Fruits or veggies, pureed	1 cup	8.5 ounces	245 grams
Honey, maple syrup, or corn syrup	1 tablespoon	0.75 ounce	20 grams
Liquids: cream, milk, water, or juice	1 cup	8 fluid ounces	240 milliliters
Oats	1 cup	5.5 ounces	150 grams
Salt	1 teaspoon	0.2 ounce	6 grams
Spices: cinnamon, cloves, ginger, or nutmeg (ground)	1 teaspoon	0.2 ounce	5 milliliters
Sugar, brown, firmly packed	1 cup	7 ounces	200 grams
Sugar, white	1 cup/1 tablespoon	7 ounces/0.5 ounce	200 grams/12.5 grams
Vanilla extract	1 teaspoon	0.2 ounce	4 grams

OVEN TEMPERATURES

Fahrenheit	Celsius	Gas Mark
225°	110°	¼
250°	120°	½
275°	140°	1
300°	150°	2
325°	160°	3
350°	180°	4
375°	190°	5
400°	200°	6
425°	220°	7
450°	230°	8

Index